STUDIO
BASICS

STUDIO BASICS

WHAT YOU SHOULD KNOW  ENTERING THE RECORDING STUDIO

RICHARD MANSFIELD

BILLBOARD BOOKS
An imprint of Watson-Guptill Publications/New York

R

Senior Editor: Bob Nirkind
Edited by: Ginny Croft
Book and cover design: Bob Fillie, Graphiti Graphics
Production Manager: Ellen Greene

First published 1998 by Billboard Books,
an imprint of Watson-Guptill Publications,
a division of BPI Communications, Inc.
1515 Broadway, New York, NY 10036

Library of Congress Cataloging-in-Publication Data
Mansfield, Richard.
    Studio basics: what you should know before entering the
recording studio/Richard Mansfield
       p. cm.
    Includes bibliographical references (p. 155–158) and index.
    ISBN 0-8230-8488-4
    1. Sound—Recording and reproducing. 2. Sound studios.
    3. Sound recording—Production and direction. I. Title
TK7881.4.M367   1998
781.49—dc21   97–46341
                            CIP

Manufactured in the United States of America.

First printing, 1998

1 2 3 4 5 6 7 8 9 / 06 05 04 03 02 01 99 98

ACKNOWLEDGMENTS

I'D LIKE TO THANK Marc Wintriss for his noblesse oblige while introducing me to the recording process. Dave Kesner, recording engineer at UCSD, was extremely generous with his time; his suggestions were right on. And Libby Stewart deserves recognition for her saintlike patience in editing yet another of my somewhat trying texts, though she don't always like the way they's a-writ. Thanks to Dean Kamei for encouraging me to give this project a shot. Very special thanks to Sallie Bayless for making the key suggestion that I simply send the manuscript directly to the right people instead of taking my usual, somewhat circuitous approach. Clearwater Writing is, in part, responsible for tempering my enthusiasm for commas.

As usual, I've depended on the help of people who barely know me but have always treated me like a friend. They are Charlie Musselwhite, Patrick Ford of Blue Rock'it Records, and fingerpicker Dale Miller. Bruce Iglauer of Alligator Records, thanks for always taking the time to respond personally.

Thank you, Dick Shurman; Blair Hardman of Zone Recording Studios in Cotati, California; Jeff and Suzanne Forrest of Doubletime Productions (San Diego); Dave Wellhausen (in San Francisco); and Tad Dowd, for unwittingly allowing me occasional small glimpses into the workings of the industry exec's mind. Thanks to all the recording studio professionals who submitted to full-length interviews, answered my questions over the phone, or took the time to fill out the questionnaire and shoot it back to me. Mark Putnam, of Avocado Records, Marc Allyn, and Chris Camp were the first to offer their advice. The big guy at Moonlight Music in Encinitas was kind enough to answer an almost endless stream of seemingly idiotic questions, from a stranger, over the phone. Reference librarians are, or course, some of the finest people around and there are none better than in Encinitas and Vista.

It has been, for some time now, my great good pleasure to work with blues musicians. Like any other segment of society, they represent a wide variety of character types, personal problems, and neuroses, but they all share one thing. The single common characteristic I've experienced, almost unfailingly, in these people (whether they've made it, or are livin' the life) is generosity. The best musicians—meaning the most highly respected by their peers—have always proven to be the most generous. I've found this to be so consistently true that when I meet a musician who lacks generosity I assume that person is not a very good musician, which usually proves to be so. The musicians I've met are especially generous when it comes to their fellow musicians. When criticism of one musician comes from the mouth of another, it is usually good-natured, understated, or cast in the courtesy of euphemism. To me that's a remarkable, admirable way to live. That the best music comes from the heart is a proven reality, as far as I can determine.

Musicians are remarkable in their ability to swim around casually in the social milieu, seemingly unjostled by it in any way. They are seriously bruised, however, by the continual lack of recognition of their artistry. So I want to take this opportunity to thank every musician whose music has ever gotten me up doing my personal, awkward, embarrassing imitation of what someone once might have mistaken for dance. If you've taken the time to talk with me, I hope I've represented you well. Believe me, it has been an honor to find myself in a position where I can talk with someone whose music has reached me. Your music has washed over my soul and made me a better man.

I also need to thank all the good people in the blues community, who have continually and consistently proven themselves to be the finest human beings on the face of this planet. Somebody, pass the ribs.

CONTENTS

PREFACE

I've been through parts of many recording sessions as an invited observer, but it wasn't until the fall of 1993 that I found myself on the other side of the glass for the first time. One night, long after midnight, I sat propped up nervously on a barstool, my instrument clenched in my sweaty palms, while the recording engineer adjusted the microphone to within inches of the bridge. I was awash in fear but also anxious just to get things underway. It felt pretty much the same as being in the dentist's chair waiting for a molar extraction.

Before a single note was struck, I was already having serious doubts.

Then, when the headphones went on, things got *really* peculiar. I could hear my own breathing; I could feel my heartbeat. When I adjusted my feet on the rung of the barstool, the sound was amplified and fed back to me instantaneously in crystal-clear, gritty stereo. The dryness of my fingertips on the surface of the strings was blatant, glaring, undeniable. The thought that *that* sound would be recorded too rankled nearly as much as the sound itself.

I'd never played with a microphone poised so close to my hands before, and I was concerned about how it might restrict my technique. But naturally I was too nervous to say anything. Instead I decided to play the best I could with my hand in an awkward new, completely foreign position, in order to accommodate the mic. When the talkback clicked on and the engineer asked me to play something, I was so nervous I stammered, "What do you want me to play?" He clicked on again, "Anything." That struck me as humorous, because "anything" was precisely what I couldn't think of at that moment.

After a couple bars of scales, he reappeared in the studio to readjust the microphone. This time he positioned it directly in front of the sound hole—where all the flailing takes place—which, of course, made my task even more difficult. I was gravely aware of the horrendous noise a live microphone makes when bumped. Luckily, this positioning didn't work out either. When he came out to readjust the mic a third time, I asked nervously if there was anything I could do to help. He said, a little peevishly, "Just sit there." So I did. I just sat there.

After what seemed like hours of testing, the talkback clicked on and he said, "OK, let's give it a try." The rush was so heavy that my mind went blank. I was rendered incapable of thought. Although by now I had a tune in mind, I literally could not recall which string to start out on. And I couldn't relax enough to simply dive into it as I normally would. Trying to think my way through only seemed to confuse matters. I tried several different approaches, and they all sounded, not just wrong, but seriously wrong. After two or three notes I'd quit, exhale loudly into the microphone, and try to regroup. I really wondered what I was doing there. It was pretty clear that I was lost. But it took me a while to admit to it. Finally I leaned into the mic and confessed, "Uh . . . I don't know what to do."

The engineer offered assurance and encouragement from the booth, but somehow that only added to the pressure. He suggested that I count off the beat. But I'd never counted off a beat in my life, and attempting to learn then, there, on the spot, in that studio, with him looking on, proved to be not only awkward and embarrassing but also ineffectual. Suddenly I was face to face with the fact that I'd never paid any serious attention to tempo before. That seemed like kind of a huge oversight on my part, I had to admit. I'd been playing for twenty-five years, and now, suddenly, I didn't know how to get started on a tune I'd been playing for most of that time. Meanwhile, in the back of my mind, the money was spilling through the hour glass at ten times the rate I generally earn it.

If this sounds like a hellish experience, nothing could be further from the truth. Once underway, I took to the process quite naturally. I launched into a lengthy meandering ad-lib *thang* that startled me with its eloquence, even as it developed. Somehow at that moment I was gifted with the ability to ponder the notes as they hung in the air before me while at the same time plunging deliriously onward. It was quite a kick.

I was overwhelmed with the purity of the sound, fascinated by the flawlessness of my technique. My sustains were booming, my bends pure, my vibrato ice cold and more focused than ever before. As I played, predictable weary, old, worn-out phrases came back sounding fresh and new. I was delighted . . . until I heard the playback. Then it seemed like every note had an embarrassing flaw in it. There wasn't one thing about that piece that couldn't have been done better.

In my memory of that first session, everything after that first take unravels in a kind of dream time. Before I knew it, four hours had slipped away and I was sent stumbling out the door with a big grin on my face . . . and a rough mix clenched tightly in my fist. I came away from that studio absolutely ecstatic. I'd never heard my music like that before. It sounded strong, heartfelt, more playful than I ever would have guessed possible (since I'm pretty much of an old grump). And though I make no claims to being a musician, I was pleased to discover that my stuff actually sounded quite a bit like music.

The absolutely wonderful and always kindly Jack Myers—who replaced Willie Dixon as in-house bass at Chess Records—once told me something that I thought was a pretty good little story. He said that for a long time after Willie had stepped up to the role of producer, they just plain *could not* keep that man out of the studio. They'd be tracking, Jack would be on electric bass, and he'd look around to find Willie standing behind him with a beatific look on his face, thumping right along on the upright bass. Jack would look at him, like "Hey, ain't you s'posed to be in the booth?" but Willie was always too involved in the music to notice. When I met Willie Dixon a couple years later, I repeated this tale to get his reaction. He laughed loudly and said, "Yeah, a lot of times that's right."

For years I'd thought that was a story about Dixon's love for the music. But after my own first session, I suddenly understood it to be a story about the man's enthusiasm for recording. After having spent some time recording myself, I truly understood for the first time what a friend of mine meant when he told me, "Put food in there, and I'd *live* in the studio." I felt the same way. I couldn't wait to climb back up on that barstool again. Recording was, unqualified, one of the coolest experiences I had ever had.

While listening to the playback at the conclusion of my third session, I asked the engineer to suggest a book that might help me along a bit in the studio. "You know," I said, "just some general information so I'll feel a little more comfortable goin' in."

He said, "I don't know of any book like that."

I said, "Really . . . ?"

He said, "Somebody ought to write a book like that."

I said, "Hmmm . . ." and began to rub my scruffy chin.

INTRODUCTION

T HE SUBTITLE OF THIS BOOK, *What You Should Know* **Before** *Entering the Recording Studio,* pretty much describes what it is about. Written with the musician in mind, it is designed to help musicians who have little or no studio experience avoid common, costly mistakes. The information found here replaces fallacies, fears, and false expectations with a basic working knowledge of what goes on in the recording studio, and why, so that the artist can go into the studio in relative comfort and come out with the best possible results.

What's interesting about recording is that, for some reason, it is one aspect of the music industry that all musicians seem to take seriously. Whatever else they may know or not know about the Biz, musicians hold an instinctual, almost reverential belief that recording is a serious matter. Unfortunately, too often their seriousness falls short of taking the necessary steps to inform themselves about the process.

Consequently, many musicians have no idea, going in, what to expect from their first studio experience. Not surprisingly, while anticipating their first session, many first-timers entertain themselves with industry-generated myths and fantasies from Empty-V, none of which are of any help once they find themselves in the studio. And too many of them comfort themselves with the illusion that recording is either just another gig or maybe a big private party. In fact, it is neither.

Recording is hard work that can be mentally, physically, and emotionally draining. When you fail to recognize the differences between recording and your usual gig, the dream has the ability to turn quickly into a nightmare. Unfortunately, misunderstandings about recording are inevitably ironed out, sometimes with crushing results, through the recording process itself. This book was written to help the first-timer avoid such crushing reality and possibly even fulfill the dream.

Anyone who has been in a recording studio for any length of time, on either side of the glass, knows how fulfilling the process can be. That person also knows it can become tedious, drawn out, and frustrating for all parties involved. But there is a reason that things sometimes get that way. And many problems can be avoided when the artist recognizes certain basic realities.

Recording and *performance* are two very distinct experiences. They are, in fact, worlds apart. Everything you may rely on in performance—spontaneity, improvisation, audience response, accompaniment, the ability to move around on stage, showmanship, and other factors that feed life into performance—are all purposefully, necessarily, and strictly absent in the recording studio.

Not only is much of what you have learned on stage rendered useless in the studio, but the studio is more demanding. It's also less forgiving. Consequently, the pressure to perform is far greater in the studio than on stage. For example, if you play through mistakes on stage, they are soon forgotten, but on tape mistakes refuse to be forgotten and cannot be ignored until they are remedied.

Additional pressure is added by the fact that the "audience" in the studio is not an audience at all. They are not a gaggle of close, personal friends, not a bunch of drunken, dedicated fans, but a somewhat sober team of highly paid, highly trained, highly perceptive, sometimes highly strung professionals, and they are not there to be entertained. They're not there to make new friends. They're not there to fawn over the musician's artistry or laugh at anyone's jokes. They are there to work. Their position demands that they cast a pretty cold eye on the task.

We're told that the number-one complaint by music industry professionals is that artists simply do not understand the structure and workings of the Biz. That problem is exemplified, of course, in the studio. Recording studio professionals are, at times, convinced that no one understands their craft, least of all the musicians with whom they find themselves working. What's peculiar in this equation is that most recording studio professionals have backgrounds as musicians themselves and thereby have some insight into the demands of performance. Perhaps that's why they work so hard to turn musical straw into recorded gold for people they feel may not fully appreciate their efforts.

The difference between the artist and the studio professional cannot, I think, be overemphasized. The trained personnel who work in and around recording studios are, by nature, extremely meticulous, analytical folk and necessarily so. Musicians, on the other hand, are sometimes exactly the opposite. Stick these two in a confined space together for long hours, handling a tightly focused, sometimes tedious task, and the results are almost predictable. Yet that is precisely the situation in the recording studio.

The difference between the studio professional and the musician is not always as simple as the difference between quantitative and qualitative, but there is much of that to it. Engineers are fond of saying things like "My job is to capture a memorable performance." But when asked what constitutes a memorable performance, their eyes go flat, their voice takes on a robotic tone, and they start reciting data about EQ, dB headroom, and signal-to-noise ratios. In contrast, a working musician, when asked what constitutes a memorable performance, is likely to blurt out something about one night in Pocatello when some blonde's enraged boyfriend climbed on stage, mid-tune, brandishing a meat cleaver.

From the engineer's point of view, the most mindless musical mayhem can be recorded satisfactorily, and its aesthetic value and commercial viability simply do not factor in. It is not the engineer's job to recognize musical blunders, nor to judge or critique performance. The engineer's job is to record whatever goes on—no matter how ethereal or embarrassing—and to do it accurately, cleanly, and with as much gain and separation as possible so that the final mix will retain punch, depth, and clarity. The musician is in there to make history, at least of a personal sort if not on a somewhat grander scale.

Even the producer, whose job it is to make music-based decisions, is bound primarily to the recording process, not to the music per se. Whether the horn section stinks or not, the producer sees that they surface when they should and slip down quietly underneath when that's expected. Finally, it's the producer's job to see that the project runs well to completion. The musician's focus on such matters is typically (and correctly, I should add) confined to each individual take.

There are lessons to be learned about the recording process itself that time and experience alone can deliver. The first is that things in the studio are not always what they seem. In the studio things occur that are surprising, unpredictable, unexplainable, and sometimes, apparently, even impossible. Only experience allows anyone to make sense out of them. But even experience is no guarantee. The president of a major label admits that, even after years of in-studio experience, "It's *all* kind of strange." The strangeness of it all is usually driven home each time the talkback clicks on and a distant, tinny voice from out of nowhere gives you a seemingly random command to stop, stand by, or try it again.

Playback consistently drives home the simple fact that what the musician hears, or seems to hear, and what is being recorded often are not the same thing at all. For example, during tracking, mistakes that sound just absolutely horrendous through the headphones sometimes turn out not to be so bad after all. When your fingers rebel and independently decide to attempt a new, untried, never-before-even-imagined phrase (instead of the one they've been practicing since childhood), sometimes it's a remarkable success. Some subconsciously inspired innovations turn out to be miracles. Other times, when you feel like you're really tearing the place apart, playing like a demon—you've never played better in your entire life; you're grinding out a solo that rocks the room like a thundering, fully loaded freight train—playback may reveal that monumental onslaught for what it actually was: overly mechanical, flat, contrived, or just plain out of control.

Whereas it is understandable that the tape may show you're not playing as badly as you think, it's somewhat more difficult to understand why, if you think you're playing great, the tape doesn't confirm it. Such occurrences, however, are not unusual in the studio. In fact, they are typical.

That's why, whatever the musician's aspirations going in, any first-timer can end up in trouble. Without warning, you may find yourself struggling, frustrated, possibly even a little frightened by what is going on. You may have no idea how you got into the mess and absolutely no idea how to extract yourself. In short, you may find yourself bewildered by the process.

When things begin to unravel in the studio, you may begin to doubt your own abilities, especially if others seem to be handling things more easily. But knowledge about, and comfort with, the recording process comes with time. Problems in the studio are not usually a reflection of some glaring weakness in musicianship—many are merely a reflection of lack of experience. Experience has a lot to do with how smoothly recording sessions work themselves out.

Even with experience, problems in the studio never go away entirely. In a very real sense, problems *are* the process. Of course, that news offers little comfort to the first-timer cast suddenly in the midst of a recording studio horror show. And the fact that experienced recording artists also find themselves struggling from time to time offers little hope. The difference is that experienced recording artists accept the process for what it is.

One advantage experienced recording artists have over first-timers—though they, too, may continue to find the recording experience unnerving—is that they *know* that asking questions and making their needs known are both integral parts of getting the results they're after. First-timers, however, usually hesitate to ask questions, which only complicates matters.

Not surprisingly, the first-timer who may be uncomfortable to begin with, and having trouble performing, can feel tremendous pressure to remain mute. Any musician who is aware of the ticking of the clock is reluctant to bring things to a grinding halt and attract attention by asking what might sound like a silly question. Consequently, from the studio's perspective, the first-timer may seem, at times, not only incapable of delivering a good performance but also incapable of expressing what it is he or she wants. As anyone in any trade will tell you, if the client can't express what they want, you can't give it to them.

Recording studio professionals, like professionals in any field, do not always enjoy working with amateurs. In fact, many studio professionals simply refuse to work with first-timers. And justifiably so. The work is hard enough without all the problems first-timers bring into the studio. It can be frustrating to have to explain everything to a client who does not understand or even pretend to care about your craft.

Recording engineers, producers, and sound technicians do occasionally become detached, bored, sullen, stubborn, and even belligerent. Generally, however, the forbearance of engineers and studio personnel is remarkable. Like any other group in any other field of expertise, they cover a wide range of personality types. While some of them are saintly, others have no qualms about expressing their waning expectations in the artist's ability to deliver.

It's not the studio professional's job to offer instruction about how to avoid predictable mistakes in the studio. Traditionally, they take a hands-off attitude when it comes to things like aesthetic judgment. It's not their job to shatter illusions, correct delusions, or offer career advice. When they do, they set themselves up for the classic quandary: they've offered good advice, but the musician simply refuses to take it. Musicians at every level are notorious for taking this (somewhat justifiable) stance when it comes to advice. Bear in mind, however, that the performers who make it in the music industry invariably surround themselves with an entire team of experts and always listen carefully to the advice these experts offer.

Once you've booked the studio, there is no turning back. At that point there is nothing anyone can do to help if you are not prepared. To learn as you go, while in the studio, is an all too common but costly course. It's costly not only in time and money but in results as well. If you go in unprepared, the best engineer in the world may not be able to extract good music from the dregs.

Throughout all of this, you are the one who is wandering into strange territory. You are the one who needs to become informed about what to expect, what is expected of you, how to conduct yourself, and how to get what you're after. The artist who goes into the studio knowing which is his ass and which is first base has a decided advantage and will probably gain a little special consideration as well. It's not the engineer's job to draw you a diagram. That is, however, the job of this book.

Although a lot of what is found herein may seem obvious to some, it's amazing *how obvious it ain't* to first-timers. Necessarily, then, this is not a technical manual. For the artist it's more important to arrive on time, with your gear in order, your repertoire together, and with some idea of what to expect, than it is to arrive with a head full of technological terminology.

Being properly informed about what to expect in the studio is part of being properly prepared and important to the task of getting successful results. Ultimately, as an artist you'll benefit from *any* information you may gather about the recording process. The time to do that, of course, is *before* going into the studio.

In recording, as in any other human endeavor, there is an inside and an outside. Inside there is a shared understanding about what's going on, how things work, and why. Inside there is a lexicon, a hierarchy, and an expected decorum. Outside there are mostly useless, even some crazy, ideas about how things work on the inside. If you are going to step inside the recording world, for whatever reason, it will not hurt to have some concept (based at least partly in reality) about how the recording process works.

There are benefits to looking, acting, and sounding like you know what you're doing. Professionals in any field are more likely to do good work for people they feel understand their task. So by learning something about the studio before going in, you will ingratiate yourself to the producers, engineers, and sound technicians you'll be dealing with.

Wisdom, however, is sometimes best conveyed in silence, especially while others are working. Studio personnel will have a greater respect for someone who demonstrates a quiet understanding of what it takes to mic an instrument and get everybody's playback set up, than for anyone, no matter how knowledgeable, who interferes in these tasks. This rule applies to every aspect of the process for the duration of the project. In almost every situation in life, a respectful silence is always appreciated more than the grating sound of someone who clearly doesn't know what the hell he or she is talking about. That's especially true in the recording studio.

Mark Twain said something to the effect that it's better to keep your mouth shut and have people think you may be an idiot than to open it and confirm the fact. This advice is perfectly suited for anyone going into the studio for the first time. Another genius, Albert Einstein, shared the same point of view. When asked for a formula for success, he came up with this: WORK + PLAY + KEEP YOUR MOUTH SHUT = SUCCESS.

What I'm advising throughout this book is that you learn the basics so that when you go into the studio you don't feel overwhelmed or lost. I'm advising you to ask questions. I'm advising you to make your needs known. I am *not* advising that you learn a lot of studio jargon and hang around in the booth spouting off. In fact—just to be clear—I'm advising against that. Miles Davis said it succinctly: "Avoid unnecessary bullshit." That means don't generate it either. In this case brevity is not only the soul of wit; it's the soul of wisdom.

THE RECORDING STUDIO QUIZ

The following quiz touches on some of the words you may come into contact with while in the recording studio. Go through the list quickly and see how many answers you have already at hand. If much of this leaves you totally flummoxed, it would probably be a good idea for you to settle in and do some reading. Conveniently enough, the very book you hold has some of the answers you may be seeking.

Questions

1. What is wow?

2. What is flutter?

3. What is magneto-optical?

4. What is ducking?

5. What is keying?

6. When you're done recording, who owns the master?

7. Where is it stored and in what format?

8. When you're done, what format should you ask for?

9. Can you record at home as well as you can in the studio on a $600,000 board?

10. What is punching in?

11. What is crosstalk?

12. What is talkback?

13. What are sweeteners?

14. What is the dynamic range?

15. What does a studio musician (session player) do? Where do you find such a person?

16. What are the payment arrangements for studio musicians?

17. Do they get royalties?

18. When is a vocalist not a vocalist?

19. What are mechanical rights?

20. What is the difference between a sound recording and a phonorecord?

21. Whom does the producer work for?

22. What is RIAA?

23. How much degeneration can you expect digitally from one generation to the next?

24. What does the sound engineer do?

25. What is a block-out?

26. What are all those knobs about?

27. How many ways are there to properly mic a drum set? How long can you expect to spend micing a drum set?

28. What is amplitude?

29. What is cross-fade?

30. What is preproduction?

31. What is the studio's investment in your work once it's been mastered?

32. How much money should you budget toward microphones for your home studio?

33. Explain briefly how a harmonics filter, which is made up of fourth-order subfilters and fed from a phase-inverted side chain taken from the subbass network, can be utilized to inversely set the starting frequency of the harmonic filter in the mid to high range.

Answers

1. Wow is a sound distortion that occurs when audiotape becomes stretched due to a malfunction of a recording machine. It's much like the sound that a wah-wah pedal produces.

2. Flutter is a sound distortion caused when audiotape fails to make good head contact. It's a chattering sort of effect. If you are buying 2-inch tape for your session, be aware that the longer spool carries thinner tape, which is more likely to suffer these kinds of problems. The trade-off is possibly losing valuable takes because the short reel runs out.

3. Magneto-optical is an alternative storage medium using recordable CDs. Its only advantage seems to be that the recorders are small (the one I had was slightly smaller than a portable CD player) and the disks are relatively inexpensive.

4. Ducking is the fading of other channels whenever a specific channel is activated. For example, if you do not want all those horns in there while the lady's trying to sing, the engineer ducks the horns underneath during her rendition.

5. Keying is similar to ducking, but the undesired channels or tracks are cut entirely while the *key* channel is tracking (recording).

6. When you're done, the master belongs to you.

7. If you're lucky, the master will be stored somewhere other than in your apartment, in some digital form. It's not unusual for studios to store archival copies of sessions done at their facility for the duration of their business relationship with you. That's how, twenty years after some artist is dead and all of his or her recordings supposedly issued, someone may discover new songs by that artist. Those new songs are typically archival copies or out-takes that had been buried in the tape stacks at some studio.

8. When you're done, you should ask for one analog (cassette) version and one digital version. The analog version is readily duplicated (by you when you need a copy), while digital is the choice of people in the Biz.

9. Many musicians think you can. Some tiny, upstart independent labels think you can. No industry pros think you can.

10. Punching in is playing along with a track up to the point where you've screwed up on a previous take; at that point you continue to play while the engineer *punches in* your improved version on top of that screw-up. At the end of the correction, the engineer *punches out*. In playback—if things go perfectly—your new improved take of that little passage will fit seamlessly where the screw-up used to be.

11. Crosstalk is the seepage of sound between recorded tracks due to electron-

ic/mechanical problems with the micing, the console, or tape deck. *Leakage* between tracks is the result of microphones picking up stray sound.

12. The talkback is the device through which the engineer and the musician in the studio can hear each other.

13. Sweeteners (or sweetening) are tracks cut usually after your basic tracks and commonly after the vocals. They are highlight motifs, typically produced by horns or strings, sometimes by unusual percussion instruments, brought in specifically for that purpose.

14. The dynamic range is the range of sound from loud to soft that recording equipment, tape, microphones, and the like are capable of carrying without distortion. All such electronics are rated by their dynamic range.

15. Studio musicians, or session players, are brought in for various reasons, for example, to correct mistakes that are simply beyond the recording artist's ability, to add sweetener, or to elevate the tune to a level of commercial viability, competence, pop appeal, or professionalism. Such a person might be found through the musicians' union. There are restrictions as to who can hire them, what instruments they can play, how long they can play, and how they are to be compensated.

16. They are paid at the end of their work.

17. They get no royalties.

18. According to the musicians' union, any vocalist who also plays an instrument is not a vocalist (and therefore not paid at the vocalists' rate) but a mere musician (and therefore paid at the lesser rate).

19. Mechanical rights are the rights to reproduce and sell a sound recording of another person's copyrighted work.

20. A sound recording is, for example, the master of your work in the studio, no matter who owns the rights to the individual pieces recorded. A phonorecord is the recorded documentation of an original tune or tunes for copyright purposes.

21. The producer may be working for you directly, working independently, or working for a record company. No matter which is the case, you are responsible for seeing that he or she is paid.

22. RIAA is the Record Industry Association of America. They keep tabs on marketing and sales and actively combat bootlegging and piracy.

23. None. Digital stuff is stored in numbers, and numbers (for the most part) do not change. In digital, degeneration is minimal. Analog recording—where sound is stored on metallic particles suspended on a film—degrade with each transference (generation) and even lose a little just sitting around rolled up in storage.

24. The sound engineer's goal is to do everything necessary to see that your work is recorded with depth, clarity, and separation. In the mix it's the engineer's job to see that those same factors remain in place. In order to get there, he or she oversees all the technical aspects of recording: mic selection, console, recorder and outboard gear operation.

25. A block-out is a block of time in the studio. "OK, let's block out Saturday, Sunday, and Monday at 3 A.M." A *lock-out* means the studio is booked and unavailable, typically 24 hours a day for several days or weeks.

26. If anybody knows what all those knobs are about, it's the engineer. Forget the knobs, concentrate on *your* job.

27. There are whole schools of thought on micing techniques, different philosophies—all conflicting. Someone will tell you that it takes six microphones to mic a drum set. Someone from L.A. may tell you that Led Zepp uses only four. Some will say it's good to split the over and under mics on the snare to separate tracks. Others would dispute that. The key to micing, ultimately, is control. What you're after is separation, depth, punch. Done properly, it can take forever. Done improperly, it takes considerably less time but doesn't sound as good.

28. Amplitude is the volume knob.

29. Cross-fade occurs when, for example, the vocals drop underneath and, at the same time, the guitar surfaces smoothly.

30. Preproduction is everything you should do before striking the first note and a few things you should do before each subsequent session.

31. Most studios have no real investment in your work at all, but they *are* invested in how their own work comes across, which is linked inextricably with your work. That is why you can expect them to do the best job they are capable of doing.

32. Buying top-of-the-line recording equipment accomplishes nothing if you feed it with a cheapo mic.

33. A harmonics filter, which is made up of fourth-order subfilters and fed from a phase-inverted side chain taken from the subbass network, can be utilized to inversely set the starting frequency of the harmonic filter in the mid to high range by someone who understands such stuff. Not by me, not by you. And that's really OK. In the studio you'll continually be dependent on the expertise of others. Initially, the less you resist that fact, the easier it will go, and the better the results of your hard work will be.

1

HOME RECORDING
AND
STUDIO RECORDING

O N THE SURFACE IT MAY appear that home project studios and professional recording studios are competitive ventures. That's a common misunderstanding. In reality, home recording and in-studio recording are different processes using different equipment, and the products cannot be compared. Whatever anyone may tell you, the home project studio is no competition for the professional recording studio.

They are, however, supplementary processes that can work very nicely together. That's why most studio professionals encourage musicians to spend as much time as they can recording at home. The best time to learn about the recording process is *before* entering the studio. That way you are not paying a sound engineer to explain things to you while the meter's running. Learning while in the studio is a common but expensive way to go.

Because they have heard the phrase "We can fix it in the mix," some musicians think the studio can, through the magic of technology, transform a tape they've done at home into a professional recording. But it can't be done. Because of relatively inexpensive electronic components, even the best home recording equipment produces, by industry standards, a pretty noisy tape. There is simply no way that a device that sells off-the-shelf for a couple of grand can deliver the same results as several hundred thousand dollars' worth of professional studio equipment. If there were, professional studios would gladly forgo the expense themselves.

Musicians are sometimes also confused by industry myths about some part of a Grammy-winning song being recorded in the artist's bathroom or closet. If there is any truth behind such tales—and sometimes there is—it's not the whole truth. What's left out is the fact that the tune was recorded with top-of-the-line microphones, run through a state-of-the-art board, and taped on the most extreme high-end tape machine available, all nestled nicely in the artist's custom-built home studio. That's why if you tape the exact same thing, note for note, using lesser equipment, it is going to sound like it was recorded in a bathroom or a closet . . . and it probably won't win any awards.

Of course, with the advent of modular digital multitrack systems such as ADAT (and other similar equipment), the gap between professional and semi-professional equipment has narrowed considerably. At this writing, newer formats are emerging that narrow the gap even further. But whatever the quality of home recording equipment (and whatever its cost), the professional recording studio continues to give you something you cannot attain at home: a staff of skilled, experienced professionals providing expert guidance throughout the project. Unfortunately, many first-timers either resist or ignore such guidance. The wise thing, of course, for any neophyte to do in any situation is to be flexible, observe quietly, and absorb as much as possible.

HOME RECORDING AS A REHEARSAL TOOL

Home recording is a great rehearsal tool. It is perfect for working out new ways to present old tunes. And it's more suited for experimentation and just plain noodling around than even the cheapest recording studio. Additionally, home recording is *superior* to studio recording when it comes to capturing those spontaneous bursts of genius that otherwise might be lost. In fact, many professionals use home recording for just this purpose.

Frankly, many musicians (professionals and amateurs alike) find the studio environment so intimidating that such inspired performance may never emerge in studio sessions. In fact, such spontaneity is discouraged by the process itself. Still, everyone knows that sometimes ad-libs, or even mistakes, turn out to be the best thing you get on tape. How to get such inspired stuff into the studio is the challenge. The answer is to capture it at home and work it into your routine.

Captured at home, such inspiration can be played back, worked on, learned, and incorporated into your routine. Then later, in the studio, it can reappear skillfully presented as part of your repertoire (see "Routining," page 00).

Two successful professional musicians offer words of advice on home recording. Fingerpicker Dale Miller says:

Investing in a four-track is really worth the money. I remember in one of my recording projects I got this $400 four-track and it saved me all kinds of money. For every session I did with people who weren't studio experienced, I brought them to my house first and we went through a dress rehearsal with the four-track. That's something I think really helps. Even if you do not have a tape recorder, put phony mics in front of people and do a total dress rehearsal. Otherwise, they never know what it's going to be like. Also, don't treat home recording as *just home recording*. In other words, use the same procedure as you would in the studio: "Take one. . . . Take two. . . ." And if you're going to bring in a musician to overdub in the studio, bring him in and have him put on headphones at your house. Do it just like in the studio.

Blues statesman Charlie Musselwhite concurs:

I just recently got one of those little home tape recorders—it's like a four-track thing. I have barely used it at all, but it's got a lot of possibilities. I look forward to working with it. I think it's a real good way to get your ideas across to other musicians. First of all, you can experiment with your own ideas to see if they really work. If you play more than one instrument, you can lay down a rhythm track and a bass track and the lead over the top of that. You can see how the chords work with the melody you have in mind— all those kind of things—without having to hire a whole band.

In the past, the only time I would use a tape was when I heard an example of something I was looking for. I'd make a copy of it so I could say, "Now, here, see how that bass line goes? I think that's close to what I want." Or "The tone, the tone of the guitar—can you get me that tone?" Or that kind of attack or rhythms. "I like the way the drummer is carrying that rhythm" or the way he does his accents. That was the only way I could give examples of what I was trying to say, since I'm not a drummer. It's a way of exchanging ideas.

Sometimes, if we're just rehearsing, just foolin' around, and some kind of a groove comes up, I'll tape it. And I'll take that tape home and I'll work with that tape. It will trigger some sort of words that I can hear that will go with it, and I'll work with that. I'll shape it into something and then, maybe, it will become a tune later on. Sometimes it goes on to be something completely different from what went on the tape in the jam session.

The recording studio is not a rehearsal studio. Do your rehearsing at home. When you go into the studio, you do not want to waste time. You want to go in well rehearsed, your repertoire routined, ready to record.

THE STUDIO PROCESS

The studio process works best as a method for capturing repertoire. Since studio time is expensive and typically booked in short, limited blocks, it's only sensible to stick with what you know and what you are in there to do. Consequently, once you cross the threshold of the recording studio, the noodling comes to an end. The experimentation must stop. When you enter the studio, the way you plan to present each tune should be solidly established (routine) and the time to make any changes was yesterday.

If you have spent a lot of time recording at home, you may actually need a little re-education before going in. If you make decisions in the studio based on your home-recording experience, those decisions may be wrong. Specifics can be quite different in the studio. In fact, some things are just the opposite of what you may have come to expect. For example, with home recording you can usually attain better results if you turn up the volume on your amp or on the instrument itself, rather than trying to control that through the board. In the recording studio the exact opposite is usually true.

Other things may be different as well. If you're used to micing your guitar amp—one mic real close, one three feet away for ambient sound—you may discover they will set you up differently in the studio to get similar (or better) results. The point is to tell the staff the kind of sound you're after, not how to go about getting it. This fine differentiation can make all the difference in the world when it comes to how things go for you in the studio.

Noise reduction can cause problems if you're used to recording at home. For some reason or other, noise reduction is one of those topics about which everyone has an opinion and too many think they are experts. Generally, the higher the tape speed and the wider the tape, the less need there is for noise reduction. And in the studio you will probably be tracking at higher speed, on wider tape, than you would be at home. Common wisdom is, noise reduction should be used in playback only, if at all. But in the studio that's *their* decision.

In the professional recording studio, what is going on in the booth and what's going on in the studio are frequently separate and unrelated. So the artist who is used to working at home needs to stay in contact with the booth. Just because you're playing doesn't mean that tape is rolling. There is nothing worse than to lay out a perfect, elusive, timelessly beautiful, melodic line, finish up with a solemn prolonged silence (and then that irrepressible sheepish grin), only to hear the engineer click on to say, "OK, any time you're ready."

If you're used to throwing all the switches—being performer, producer, recording engineer, sound technician, and gofer—turning over the reins can be a problem. Suddenly your role is reduced to a single task and, somewhat more problematic, you are expected to rely on other people's judgment. At times it can be difficult to walk the line between defending the integrity of your music and doing what's best for the project. Your work—tunes you've created and hammered into flawless form—are now in the hands of someone you may not even know. Whatever your instincts, it's better all around if you are cooperative and do what you're asked to do.

If you can arrange it, go in while someone you know is recording. Watch and absorb. Notice that everybody has a definite role. It's the engineer's job to notch some stuff out of the way when there's too much low frequency masking the mid range. It's the producer's job to say, "OK, that's good enough, let's move on." Your job is to hit the slur in the coda perfectly. Anything beyond that could be seen as meddling.

Inevitably, you will need to submit to the way the professional recording studio is run. That means, to a large degree, you'll need to learn to stay out of matters that are being handled by others. As a general rule, any time you leave the studio to go into the control room, you slow things down, cause unnecessary delay, and possibly even piss people off. You do not want any of that. So stay put, focus on your job, and let others focus on their tasks without interference. The engineer is not going to come bursting into the studio, yank your instrument out of your hands, and say, "Here, let me show you how it's done." Conversely, you shouldn't be telling the engineer how to work either. To be concerned only with playing your music is a luxury. Enjoy it. Putting yourself totally in someone else's hands can free your mind, if you will allow it.

Part of what you are paying for in the professional recording studio is the expertise of the studio personnel. You should rely on their judgment. Unfortunately, performing artists of every sort, at every level, are notorious for paying professionals for their expert advice, then refusing to take the advice these paid professionals offer. In the studio, try to be receptive to advice offered by others.

Generally, when you hound professionals into giving you what *you* want—against their informed, better judgment—it's a mistake. Things turn out badly, and it's a waste of time. In the studio it's not always easy to recognize such situations because the studio staff will usually yield to the demands of the artist—who, after all, is paying the bills. But the artist who insists on having his or her way when the studio professional advises against it usually, eventually, ends up submitting to the professional's original suggestion. Consequently, everything in the interim was just a needless waste of time.

If you're going to pay somebody good money for their wisdom, at least consider what they have to say.

HOME RECORDING AS A PREPRODUCTION TOOL

Home recording is perfectly suited for preproduction. The more prep you do *before* going into the studio, the easier the sessions will go and the more time you will have available to spend in the mix getting things just so. As a preproduction tool, home recording helps you to know what you sound like on tape. That should help you to judge your work critically, develop your repertoire, work out arrangements, scrap the junk, identify problems, and improve your technique. As important, it gives you some idea of the time required to get anything good recorded.

Agreement among studio professionals is unanimous when it comes to the value of home recording as a preproduction tool. Bruce Iglauer of Alligator Records explains:

Even a boom box taping will teach you a lot about your song and how it's working. If you can do a four-track cassette or something better, you'll learn whether the arrangement works, how the chord voicings fit together, and where the strengths and weaknesses of the song are. It's a hugely important tool.

Patrick Ford of Blue Rock'it Records agrees:

> Home recording is a wonderful preproduction tool that bands often neglect when they go into the studio. For example, I was producing a band and they came in without having worked out the horn parts. They had some good ideas, but they hadn't put them down in any way that they could listen back to them. So when we got in the studio, I could see lots of problems with those horn lines.
>
> Now, had they, in fact, laid these things down ahead of time, in their own homes, they'd have seen that these parts, although they were cool parts, would not work with the song in any way that was beneficial. A lot of times we work out things at the house, trying all kinds of chordal patterns and progressions, and work out all the little things before we ever get into the studio.

HOME RECORDING AND ROUTINE

Any musician who has spent any time on stage knows the importance of having the play list solidly established . . . *set*. That, in fact, is why a set is called a set. The tunes are set; the order in which they are presented is set. Traditionally, an entire performance is called a routine because the tunes are routine. The key, the tempo, the lyrics, the arrangement, the phrasing are all routine. To go out on stage without your set *routine* is only courting disaster.

The recording studio is even more demanding than live performance. Yet many musicians expect to go into the studio without the same consideration they give to their stage performance. It's a common mistake and a big one.

Many of the problems first-timers face in the studio could be eliminated if they would consolidate and routine their repertoire before going in and arrive with some understanding of how long the process may take.

To consolidate and routine your music, sit down one day and record your entire repertoire. Just lock yourself in a room and methodically grind out tunes, one after the other, until you run out of patience or time, or your fingers cramp up, or your vocal cords fail, or the cops arrive, or someone near and dear to you loses their sanity. Do not be concerned with quality, play through mistakes, do no retakes.

This long, unbroken session will give you an idea of how much time it takes just to set up, get going, and do even the poorest, most amateur job. It should also help you to understand how many tunes you can squeeze into how much time with no consideration whatsoever for quality . . . meaning no consideration for the things that take up time in the studio: mic placement, EQ, separation, soloing, roll-back, playback, retakes, orchestration, the mix. When you start to discuss booking time in a studio, you will have to give some serious thought to these matters. (See chapter 6 for a section on how to schedule studio time.)

When you run out of tunes, start in again at the top. If you run out of patience before you run out of tape, maybe the idea of going into the studio is premature. In the studio it's not unusual for first-timers to run out of both tape and patience before they have *successfully* worked through their first tune.

If you're working in a band situation, get everybody together to play your routine as you normally would on stage. When it's all finished, listen to the tape. One thing you'll learn from home recording is that *everything* is heard—fingers squeaking on the strings, breathing, inadvertent contact with the instrument's body. When you record, all of that stuff gets on tape.

When you play back what you've done, really listen to yourself. Sometimes when you're practicing, you focus on what sounds good, but in the studio it's equally important to listen for anything that might sound wrong. Always listen to your work critically. Between preproduction and final replication, you will be given many tapes of your work to listen to; always listen carefully and critically to every tape you are given. Set the time aside, focus on what you're doing, make notes. This is one habit that will pay off.

After this home recording session, seriously ask yourself these questions: How many of those tunes am I happy with? How many of them is everybody happy with? How many require retakes? If the answer to the last question isn't "all of them," then you are probably fooling yourself. That may sound cold, but if you're not ready to hear that, you are not ready to go into the studio. The studio process is unforgiving. Anything you "let slide" will probably come back to haunt you. In order to avoid that specter, begin to routine your songs now.

HOW MANY TUNES CAN YOU GET FOR 500 BUCKS?

One of the reasons people record at home is that it's so much cheaper than going into the studio. So first-timers show up at the studio with one question on their lips: "How many songs can I do for, like, five hundred dollars?" That seems like a simple enough question. But the answer is not so simple. It depends on a lot of things.

A typical mistake first-timers make is thinking that they'll go in, crank out one great, glorious, golden session, and come away with a dozen songs and an album. The reality is that you are more likely to do five sessions and come away with two or three good tunes ready to be mixed down. It's also entirely possible that you'll spend a few grueling days laboring in the studio, working steadily, working hard, doing good or even excellent work, and come away with nothing at all. It depends on the studio, the engineer, the scheduling, the cooperation of others, the phase of the moon, but most important, it depends on how well prepared you are going in. If you go in knowing what you are going to do and how you are going to do it, you've increased your odds for success tremendously.

All that aside, there are some very *real* questions you need to ask yourself before going into the studio for the first time. If you ask yourself the right questions going in, you'll save some money, some time, some embarrassment, and maybe some heartache. The up side is, you might also come away with something pretty wonderful on tape.

ARE YOU READY TO GO INTO THE STUDIO AT ALL?

The answer to that question can be found by asking yourself the following questions.

Are you capable?

That means, do you have the skills? If there is *anything* about your technique, or timing, or rhythm, or phrasing, or attack that you honestly feel could use a little more work, then you are not capable. Work those things out first.

Such problems are not going to vanish like magic when you cross the threshold into the recording studio. In fact, they will be amplified (both literally and otherwise). Any weakness in terms of musicianship will be driven home with humiliating cruelty in the studio.

Are you ready?

Can you nail each of the pieces you plan to record? The test is, do you nail it regularly and casually in practice? Do you nail it in performance? Is the arrangement routine? If you do somehow wander while playing a piece, is your understanding of it deep enough that you recover skillfully and quietly?

Setting foot in the studio will not magically endow you with the ability to play some piece that you've been futzing around with. More likely, your problems will increase exponentially. So you do not want to go into the studio with any piece that is not routine. The time to decide which version of a tune you are going to record is not while the engineer is sitting in the booth glaring at you and the 2-inch tape is rolling (see chapter 6 on song preparation).

Is your equipment in order?

Has your instrument been *professionally* set up? Is it in tune, sounding good, playable? Do you have spare parts—cords, fuses, strings, tubes, back-up instruments? The wrong time to discover that you have a buzz on the fifth fret or a short in your amp or a key that sticks or a drumhead that's flat is while the clock is ticking.

Roadworthy equipment *is not* studio-worthy equipment. A lot of what you can get away with in live performance—buzzes, clicks, pops, squeaks, squeaky shoes, amplifier hum, cackling guitar cords, faulty intonation above the twelfth fret, playing slightly out of tune—you *cannot* get away with in the studio. If you are properly miced, a good engineer will capture it all for you—every lip smack, every sniffle, every rustle of your sleeve.

Is your band or accompaniment ready and capable?

Do *they* have the skills? Can *they* nail each piece? What's the state of *their* equipment? If anybody in your band is not ready, then *you* are not ready. One person's screw-up, at best, will cause delay; at worst, it will stop the project until you find a replacement who *is* capable and ready.

Do you all agree about what each piece should sound like?

Do you have routine arrangements (orchestration) for each piece? The finer your options on any given track, the finer the resultant mix. That means in the mix you do not want to be choosing between different versions of the tune (different keys, different tempos, different lyrics); you want to be choosing between different takes of the same passage. You want to be deciding which take your guitarist hit that slur in the twelfth bar most impressively. When each tune is routine, you reduce the mix to those kinds of fine decisions. Not only will the mix go easier, but you should come away with better results.

Can you speak the language?

Do you have the ability to communicate your needs and wants to the engineer? Do you have the ability to understand the engineer's perspective and what he or she is trying to accomplish for you? At almost any point in the process you may hear, in playback, sounds that simply do not sound right to you. There are reasons for that, and you will be expected to understand them . . . or at least remain respectfully quiet.

If, after answering all of the above questions, you've decided that you *are* ready to go into the studio, then an important question to ask yourself is "Why?"

WHY ARE YOU GOING INTO THE STUDIO?

This is perhaps the number-one question ignored by musicians going into the studio for the first time. *Why* are you going into the studio? What is your intent? What do you wish to get out of it? What are you going to do with the end product?

If any part of your answer includes the word *album* or *demo*, then the first word you need to take a serious look at is *budget*.

That's the first word the big boys look at. And with good reason. As one musician warns, "There are a *lot* of hidden expenses. It can be quite costly."

In recording, as in all parts of the Biz, it's best to have the biggest budget you can accumulate. When dealing with the music industry, if you do not have the bucks to do the best job possible, it's wiser to wait until you get the bucks than to put out an inferior product. Wiser by far, because money translates directly into more time, superior equipment, better musicians, a solid mix, the best mastering and duplication, good artwork, and wider distribution.

Money can be the real controlling factor, the thing that will most determine your results in the studio—more than skill, more than preparation, more than desire. (See "Budget" in chapter 6.)

Too many musicians think that they can go into the studio with a few hundred bucks and a truckload of cheap equipment, and come out with a commercially viable product. But it can't be done. Even the smallest independent labels spend $10,000 in the studio to produce an album. Major labels spend that much on demos.

The reason people in the Biz budget those kinds of figures is that it's necessary. You'll be doing yourself a favor if you bear in mind this simple fact: the executives who run the music industry are in it for the money. If it was not absolutely necessary for them to spend a quarter of a million on a record, they wouldn't. It's that simple. If they could go into a studio and grind out an album for a couple of thousand bucks, they would gladly, eagerly, do so. But they can't, and you can't either.

Remember, in the Biz you are being compared to professionals who have the bucks, who have the time, the looks, the equipment, and the connections. They have the best producers, the most highly skilled engineers, endless studio time, a highly paid, doting support staff, access to the best session players available, and the finest and most expensive recording equipment on the planet. If you can't put those same factors into play, you are not competing.

Enough time, engineering, and money *can* allow the lousiest band in the world to grind out a hit tune. It's been done before, and it will be done again. But the best band in the world, recorded badly, won't even get a listen.

Someone in the Biz (a publisher and record producer) once told me that he can *look* at a tape and tell whether it's worth listening to. I thought he was joking. But when I questioned the veracity of that statement, he assured me that he could, literally, just look at a tape and determine whether it was worth his time. Whatever your opinion of that statement, that's the mind set of the people you're dealing with.

If you're lucky enough to have a record exec make the extraordinary effort to insert your tape, then actually depress the button and cock an ear in the direction of the tape machine while your tape is running (instead of, say, having a conversation on the phone, munching on a sandwich, or pawing through some lengthy legal document), what comes out of those tiny little speakers had better be pretty remarkable. A badly recorded tape just is not gonna do it. And unless the tape *looks* like it's worth the time, it may not even make it into the machine.

The up side of all this is that going into a professional studio can make you sound a lot better than you ever have before. If you already sound great, the studio will make you sound even better. No matter how brilliant at the board, however, the studio professionals you'll be working with cannot produce miracles. They can, and usually do, give you far more than what you have paid for in terms of their expertise.

PROFESSIONAL USES OF THE TERRIBLY MISUNDERSTOOD "DEMO"

Within the music industry there are basically only two legitimate uses for a demo tape, and neither of them has anything to do with discovering new talent.

In books written by legitimate businessmen working well inside the music industry, there are rarely any other uses for demos mentioned (when they are mentioned at all).

The first use of the demo is for an *established* songwriter to get a new song to a label, publisher, personal manager, or performer who might be interested in it. Usually this involves old-school industry pros who know each other and have probably worked together in the past. Joe, a professional songwriter who has been in the Biz longer than you've been on this planet, sits down at a piano one day and plinks out a demo. He then calls Irving, who has been in the Biz since Bach first shared a cup of coffee with God in some Parisian café (probably Procope), and says, "Hey, I've got this new song. I think Annie might sound good doing it." Irv says, "OK, we're looking for some new material for her. Shoot it over to me and I'll give it a listen."

The second legitimate use of the demo within the industry is by a label that has an artist already under a development contract. They put the artist in the studio with a $5,000 or $10,000 budget to record one or two songs so that they can determine whether or not the kid has any real commercial potential, can really produce, and is worth further investment.

OVER-THE-TRANSOM DEMOS

It's true that having a demo can open doors for you on the local scene. You will discover that people who previously had no time for you suddenly start to take you more seriously once you have a good-looking, professional-sounding demo. Just having a tape that you don't have to make excuses for can give you a little boost of self-confidence. And feeling good about yourself may even help you to play a little better.

But your demo, no matter how good, means nothing to industry pros unless they have some reason to believe it might be of use to them. They have no reason to think that unless the demo comes to them through the right channels. Demos that come from industry-based lawyers, music publishers, established songwriters, established artists, other labels, A&R guys, and close personal friends who know what they're talking about are given a listen. But even those are given "about three seconds" unless the person listening has some real reason to believe it's worth the time.

Demos sent unsolicited to industry professionals are a waste of everyone's time. Agreement is unanimous, unequivocal, and unqualified on that point. Publicly, of course, it's a different song. According to the public record, every record label exec is locked in an office, putting in overtime, eagerly, jealously, methodically working through piles of tapes, looking for some future superstar. Reality is somewhat different.

Over-the-transom demos are seldom, if ever, listened to. They are either immediately tossed, stacked up in a corner somewhere to

collect dust, or if it's a quality mechanism, taken home by some underling to tape over.

For their own protection, many labels have strict rules in place about how they handle unsolicited material. In order to avoid even the possibility of debate about infringement, it's not unusual for all such tapes to be returned unopened (if you've supplied them with return postage, envelope, and labeling) or simply tossed. That way, if someone comes at them with a lawsuit, saying the label stole his or her material, they shrug and say, "That's impossible. We do not accept unsolicited material. And that which reaches us is either returned unopened or discarded."

The plain, simple, pie-in-the-face fact is that if you're planning to mail your demo to a bunch of names and numbers, no matter how legitimate the source, what you're really planning to do is distribute your demo to trash cans throughout the industry . . . and probably paying first-class postage to see that it gets there quickly.

Here's some advice from Dale Miller, an artist who has had several albums produced by different independent labels:

> I would never send an unsolicited tape. You should find a label that does the kind of music you like, and then you should call and ask, "Do you accept unsolicited tapes?" If they say yes, *then* you send them a tape. But never send it without getting the OK first. Then package it as professionally as you can. If it's just a cassette, rather than scribble the tunes on the label, print out a J-card on the computer so it has a nicer look to it. And check your cover letter for punctuation and spelling. Make it look like you've put some effort into it. Include a nice picture and a bio. Make it look as professional as possible. It's just bad manners and stupid to shotgun your tapes out.

Any time you send out something like a demo, talk to the people you will be sending it to; make sure they are interested in the kind of thing you're doing. Make sure they know your name and when to expect the package. Be sure to use the correct spelling of their names and get their titles correct. If they have expressed an interest in your work, write "Requested Material" on the bottom left corner of the mailer.

After some reasonable amount of time, call to see that the package arrived. If they do not volunteer when you might hear back, don't ask. "Just wanted to see that it got there. Thank you." Contact with people who are in a position to do your career some good should always be brief. Questions should be posed with consideration of the fact that they probably have more immediate things to tend to. No matter how innocent the intent, if a question is perceived as hounding, you've probably lost any advantage you might have previously gained. Once you have been assured they have your work, stay off the phone. Try to forget it. Move on

2

HOW TO SELECT A STUDIO

GOING INTO THE STUDIO to record your music is a pretty straightforward deal. Basically, you pay the fee and they give you the best sound possible. It's also one of the very few deals in the music Biz in which the people you're working with are really on your side. With that in mind . . .

Every studio will tell you that they have the finest, most state-of-the-art equipment available. And who knows, maybe they do. Most studios will give you a leaflet, brochure, or spec sheet that proudly details their equipment. It will delineate the make and model of the console, how many inputs to that console, how many tracks it can ultimately produce, and the make and model of the recording machines. It may also list outboard equipment—typically by name and model number—what type of monitors are used, what mics and instruments are available—for example, a grand piano or a B3. It will also state the sizes and types of studios available and whether or not each has a vocal (isolation) booth separate from the studio proper. The picture it presents can be pretty impressive.

The very real question that hovers in the shadows behind all these brilliant specs is, *what does any of this mean to you?* How are you to choose between all these wonderful studios with all this fine equipment?

If you are planning to compare specs and rate equipment, you'll find yourself in a quagmire. There is enough information and conflicting opinion out there for you to muddle around in until the end of time. Bear in mind that recording engineers study for years to obtain the necessary knowledge to run this equipment and they spend a few more hands-on years formulating their own personal, prejudicial opinion on the worthiness of any specific device. Add in the fact that even the most unworthy products available always have devoted, even rabid advocates, and where does that leave you? To complicate matters, the technology is always changing.

Studios will sometimes try to sell you on the equipment they have by saying, "This is the same console Iron Butterfly used to record 'In-A-Gadda-Da-Vida.'" Or "Throbbing Gristle uses this type of processor exclusively." Or "Deanna Durbin carried one of these microphones around in her hatbox, just in case she was overwhelmed with the sudden urge to grind out another soulful rendition of 'Oh Danny Boy' while laid over in Cincinnati."

Who knows if any of that is true? More to the point, so what? The person who says something like that probably read it in a magazine somewhere or heard it from the weasel who sold the equipment to the studio. Recording engineers usually do log such particulars so that setup for subsequent sessions will go quickly, but whether using the same microphone that Miles blew into will improve your embouchure is another matter entirely.

Surprisingly, most studios do not bother to offer a sales pitch. And when they do, it can be awkward. Don't let that run you off. You're not hiring them for their salesmanship. Even if they come across as desperate, don't mistake desperation for anything other than a desire to get work. A good desperate staff may do an excellent job for you. They may need to in order to survive.

FINDING A STUDIO

Talk to as many places as you can over the phone first. Listen to their pitches. Take notes of the way they treat you. After talking to a half-dozen studios, you'll pick up some of the lingo. Use this glimmer of knowledge to ask more specific questions on subsequent calls and decide which studios you want to go to and check out. Then go in, pry 'em open, see what's inside. The point of all this is to avoid setting yourself up for possible problems down the road if you can.

When checking out a studio, ask questions. Don't just walk in and book the joint. All recording studios are kind of a neat place to be in, but do not be misled by their grandeur. You need to get a feel for whether or not you can get some work done there. That may require a little hanging around.

Ask for their specs, of course. When they hand you the sheet, peruse it as if it might actually mean something to you. Raise one eyebrow, nod knowingly, rub your chin, and let out a little bemused chuckle, if that's your style. More important, though, talk to the people you'll be working with. See how willing they are to work with you. If they won't give you a little time beforehand, they're not going to become more generous with their time once they've cashed your check. If you get any hint that it's not possible to have a good experience recording there, go with your intuition.

Because most studios offer respectable equipment, typically the decision to use one facility rather than another ends up being based on factors that should not matter, such as the hourly fee or, worse, some other musician's recommendation.

The hourly fee is no indicator of anything. Who knows whether a low hourly fee means that the market is flooded or the owner is in desperate need to make a loan payment before his grandma loses the ancestral estate. Perhaps it *is* a sign that the studio does shoddy work.

In every aspect of the music business, the cost factor can play into getting what you're after. In general, it's advisable to spend as much money (and time) as necessary to get the best possible results. But there are cheap studios that are also great studios. A studio whose bread and butter is tape replication or some other peripheral service may charge a lower hourly rate and yet be set up to do great things. A studio like that might be glad to have the work and may welcome the opportunity. They might give your project the kind of special attention you think it demands. So don't be misled by the rate. If you like what a studio is doing and you can communicate with the staff—it may be the right studio for your project. A lot of people think, "Well, a studio is a studio," but that's not true either. Pay attention, look around, see what's coming out of there.

Dale Miller warns,

Sometimes using a studio that's not entirely professional can bounce back and hit you. That happened to me a couple of times. Earlier in my career I used studios where all sorts of noise would leak in, and for an acoustic musician that's a serious problem. But if a cheaper studio is too good a bargain, then maybe paying the price of a few fuck-ups is worth it because of the money you'll save. But I've had tapes ruined because a streetcar was going by outside. It just may not be worth the frustration.

FIGURING THE COST

Figuring the cost of the studio isn't as simple as getting an hourly rate over the phone. Rates can vary widely for different rooms and different time slots. Larger blocks of time may be progressively cheaper, and daytime blocks are usually the cheapest. There is usually a minimum for the amount of time you're required to block, and overtime is almost always charged. Ask about that for budgeting purposes. If the studio schedule allows it—meaning no one else is slated to come in directly after your session—assume a couple of hours overtime for your final session.

If you've got a limited budget, you should prepare yourself to negotiate for further discounts. Generally speaking, there is some flexibility—*if* the studio needs the work. Keep your ears open. Deals can be made. For example, if someone's got the place locked out for two weeks, you might negotiate a very good price on any remaining time in the event they finish early.

The recording studio business seems to move in waves. The studios are all booked solid for several months, and then no one's coming in. So ask when the next slack period is coming up. If it's four months down the road and you want to get into that particular studio, this will give you an opportunity to learn the primary lesson in recording: *patience.*

Check out what additional equipment may be available—drum sets, piano, synthesizer—and ask about the cost of using it. Typically such equipment is superior, always professionally set up, *and* the staff knows how to EQ and mic it.

Ask about charges and liability for leaving your own equipment in the studio between sessions. Most studios accept no liability. And be cautious. No matter how secure the place may seem (many studios appear to be built like Fort Knox), most studios are pretty wide open. A lot of people come and go carrying equipment, and no one's going to pull themselves away from what they're doing to ask, "Hey, buddy, is that your amp?"

Another musician's recommendation should be considered only if he or she has recorded something similar to the sort of thing you want to record and only if it was recorded in the manner you'd like to have your work recorded. Talk to people whose work you admire. Many performers are more than happy to talk to other musicians. If you like the sound someone is getting on record, pick up the phone. "Hey, I see that you've recorded at such-and-such studio. Tell me, how did it go? Were you happy with the way they treated you? Who did you work with there?" If everything was great, that may be more of a recommendation for the engineer than for the studio.

REAL THINGS TO CONSIDER

"Engineers are much more important than studios. If you find an engineer who has made records you like and he or she is any good, they'll be able to make most studios work for you. Don't be excited by lots of gear. The important things are a good sounding board and good mics and a GREAT engineer."—Bruce Iglauer, Alligator Records

The real factors to consider when you start looking for a studio are personnel and proximity. This may sound overly simplistic, but these are the things that count when you discover the engineer is a despot or the drummer can't make it because it's too far to drive after a full day's work trying to sell cheap knock-off perfumes to people in grocery store parking lots. Then, suddenly, the importance of the right studio personnel and close proximity becomes all too evident. It doesn't matter if a studio has the best machine in town if you can't work with the guy manning the board or it's impossible to get there.

Whichever studio you choose, a more important factor than its ability to alter pitch and tempo through top-of-the-line variable-speed recording machines, more important than the size of the microphone selection, is how good the engineer is *and* how well the two of you may be able to communicate. So meet with the engineer. Be sure he or she is the kind of person you want to be working with for hours at a time. Whatever your vision of the event, you're not going to just zip in, record, and zip right out again. You're going to be spending long, tightly focused hours working together in close contact on an important project. The task of recording is demanding enough without personality conflicts between yourself and the studio staff. Find yourself an engineer you can talk to. Even if you have very specific needs that require specialized equipment offered only by the rarest of studios, how you get along with the person who's running that equipment is a major consideration.

The importance of the engineer's temperament will become crystal clear the first time tape is rolling and your fingers decide to rebel. When your mind freezes up and your favorite tune takes on that thin, distant, foreign sound, you're not going to be worrying about whether the console is the finest custom-built SSL or something thrown together from plans found in the February '53 issue of *Hi-Fi Monthly*. When your instrument begins to squirm in your hands, you're going to want to look through the glass and see someone with something more than a cold, aristocratic glint in his eye. So find an engineer you think you might trust, someone who might give you both comfort and good advice.

How do you tell if you're dealing with the right people? Again, take note of how they treat you. Watch how they treat others. Listen to the work they've produced before.

The people you work with do not have to be diplomats. They *do* have to have an understanding of your music. Ask a professional in the field, "How do I decide on a studio?" and the answer is likely to be "What kind of things are you trying to record?" Such matters as what kind of music you play, what instruments you're using, the size of the band, the overall sound you're after, and what you plan to do with the results all factor in. The person you have asked will be thinking of producers who have done that sort of work before and which studios they've done it in. The recommendation will probably be based on those factors.

A good recommendation is the producer or engineer with a background as a working musician *playing* the instruments you're planning to record. For example, if you're recording congas, you might look for an engineer who is, or has been, a hand drummer and will be sympathetic to the kind of music you're producing. You need to feel confident that you can depend on your engineer's ears. You want someone who hears what you hear.

It's easy to determine if someone at the studio has experience recording the sound you're after. Most studios proudly display the work done in their shop. The best will sit you down and let you have a listen or send you home with a CD on loan. Does what they've produced in the past make sense to you? If you're planning to do a Beethoven medley on ocarina and they've produced Bach sonatas on pitch pipe, they may be the ones for you.

BUSINESS

Get a real understanding of the business arrangement. Find out about deposit requirements and refund policies. When is the balance due and in what form? Generally speaking, you'll be expected to pay at the end of each session and no tapes will be given until you've paid. What about studio screw-ups? If they produce an absolutely unacceptable tape, what recourse do you have? Don't hem.

Don't haw. Ask these questions directly. That way, there will be no surprises.

WHAT TYPE OF STUDIO TO LOOK FOR

Recording studios are each designed to accomplish a particular task. There are rooms built specifically with isolation in mind, where any stray sound that doesn't go directly into a mic is trapped, and there are rooms designed to record live ensemble work. Find out what types of studios are available.

There are big studios and small studios. And whatever else the ladies may tell you, gentlemen, quality has nothing to do with size. If you do not need a big room, there's no dividend in paying for one. In fact, there's much to be said for recording in an intimate setting. If it can be done that way, it's cheaper and probably a lot less intimidating.

The main thing is . . . how are you planning to record? If you're going to go in, set up, and play live, you want a room designed to capture that live sound. If you're gonna go in solo, cut dry tracks, and build your composition by overdubbing, you need a room designed with isolation in mind. If they try to convince you that one room can go either way, you might want to cock one eyebrow and look askance at them. A lively room *can* be baffled, wrapped, and padded to get the desired isolation of sound, but a room designed and constructed with that task in mind does a better job. And there's nothing you can do to get that *live* feel in a room designed and constructed to be acoustically "dead."

Patrick Ford says:

There are two really critical factors in choosing a studio—can you get a good drum sound and do you like the atmosphere? Drum sounds are very difficult to get, and the studio will make all the difference in the world. With the other instruments it's not as critical. With other instruments, because they're electrical, you have all the effects and other things you can do. But can the room get a good sound with the particular kind of drums you're going in with? It's very, very critical.

To me the second aspect is atmosphere. Is the studio a place where you can go in and be excited about being there for hours and hours on end? That doesn't mean it has to be fancy or plush. You want to go in, check the place out, thinking, "OK, I'm gonna be in here for 12 hours . . ." And all of that presupposes they have a qualified engineer.

How do you know if you can get a good drum sound there? Ford says, "They should be able to lay out for you what they've done before. They should be able to let you hear tapes of different drum sounds that were recorded there. If the studio's really cool, they'll let you set up and actually play."

DIGITAL OR ANALOG?

There are perhaps an infinite number of recording methods for any music. Apparently, for some of Robert Johnson's recordings, they simply put a cutting lathe in the next room and went right to a mother. Speaking of mothers, Frank Zappa is said to have recorded four bars at a time, doing 50 to 100 takes of each four-bar section, and mixed from there. But certain formats lend themselves to certain types of recording more than others. In these examples, Robert Johnson might have done well going direct to DAT, and Frank could probably only have done his work as he did, in the largest custom-built or drastically modified state-of-the-art studio available.

If you're looking for an answer to which is better, analog or digital, a specific answer can't be found. In terms of the end product, there seems to be a dividing line between those of us raised on analog and younger generations raised on digital. Many people raised on LPs hear something missing in digital. Maybe it's because it's recorded perfectly, but the old ear bones aren't so perfect anymore. Kids raised on CDs do not seem to detect anything wrong. Every professional digital tape deck has built-in error detection/correction circuitry. In analog that detection circuitry is called the human ear. As far as the sound is concerned, it can be only a matter of personal choice.

There are real, though personal, reasons to track to analog tape. If you just like the way it sounds, that's reason enough. Acoustic instruments sound really good on analog tape. And to a degree, analog tape is a little more forgiving. It captures more nuance, more detail in the low end. In digital, things tend to be less stable in the high end, but fidelity otherwise is unsurpassed.

The real considerations have less to do with tracking than with postproduction. Although mixing goes easily in analog, editing is difficult—almost a lost art—and there's constant degeneration to consider. With analog every transference loses a little in quality and adds a little more in distortion. From tracking to editing, mixing, mastering, and final duplication, each step loses a little. We're told that analog tape even loses a little in quality just sitting around. So it's not unusual for artists who prefer to track in analog to convert to digital immediately after tracking. You need to be aware that problems arise in any conversion, although for the most part these problems are typical and predictable (see page 00 for a description of such problems).

If you track to analog tape, for whatever reasons, mixing to a digital master is the only reasonable way to go. A DAT master is pretty much the industry standard. Within the digital realm there is almost no loss of quality from one generation to the next. And once you're mixed, no loss is exactly what you want from your chosen format.

As far as budget is concerned, if you've only got, say, $1,200 to produce a demo, the way to go may be digital. With the exception of the fact that digital is loaded into computers in real time in order to be edited (and you are charged for that time at the going rate), tracking, editing, and mastering digitally are all quicker, cleaner, neater, cheaper. Additionally, if you stay in one format, you know what you can expect to hear one generation to the next. With no conversions there are no surprises.

In digital, nothing happens by accident. One producer compares digital recording to genetic science. "You have a team of eight physicists analyzing it and working furiously to correct any flaw." Digital lends itself to that kind of endless tinkering. You have to decide, however, if that's a plus or a minus. For the artist who just wants to go in and record his work, digital can become a side track, especially if the studio staff is enthralled and entangled in the technology. A word of caution: Digital needs to be recorded at the proper sampling rate if your ultimate format is CD.

If you've got MIDI, synthesizers, and all the digital equipment to create the sound of a full-sized symphony, you're naturally going to stay in the digital realm. With that sort of thing, the variables are literally endless and you probably already know what you need in order to make that work. If you do not, don't fool with it.

DIRECT TO DAT

The way to avoid all of this, of course, is to record direct to DAT. Direct to DAT is a neat way to go because it's simple and direct. But, in general, direct to DAT is limited because everything is live-mixed to two tracks. Additionally, the format isn't convenient, or even usable to you, unless you have a DAT player.

That means your DAT recording needs to be converted to analog cassettes in order to listen to it away from the studio. And that means what you hear at home may not be representative. You need to be aware of the D/A conversion problems when you carry a copy of your work home on a cassette. The downside, or maybe it's the upside of direct to DAT is that once it's done, it's done.

"Direct to" recording demands real oversight by the producer. Before you start tracking, make sure you listen to the settings the engineer has established, because that is exactly what you're going to get. You can do several takes and choose between them, of course. However, unless a multitrack recording is made at the same time, there's no way to create separation or orchestrate or pan in the mix. Once the recording is "in the grooves," it can't be modified. That can be either scary or a tremendous relief. It depends on how the session goes.

Direct to DAT is quick, clean, neat, and efficient. It's a different technique altogether, a good option for live ensemble work. Two appropriately placed mics . . . and direct to two-track. No signal processing. If you're an acoustic soloist, going direct to DAT makes certain sense. It's also good for remote recording: no mixer, no processor, no EQ, just one or two hanging mics and go to work.

MODULAR DIGITAL MULTITRACKING

With modular digital multitracking using an analog-to-digital processor, eight channels of digital audio are stored on a VHS tape. The most touted benefit is that you can synch a dozen machines or more and get an almost limitless number of tracks. Of course, fill up all those tracks with sound and you've dug yourself a pretty deep hole. When it's time to start editing, you might as well jump on in and start pulling the dirt in over yourself. Even if your craft demands endless choices and that sort of control, there is budget to consider. As long as you have a limited budget, you probably want a limited number of takes to deal with in any format.

MDM is very cost effective for the studio, though, since each machine costs only a few grand. (There are some systems that record on 8mm videotape that are even less expensive.) For twelve grand the studio gets as many tracks as a multitrack system that might cost a quarter million dollars for the tape machine alone (reel-to-reel digital). I'm told that MDM is *nearly as clean* as any professional system out there."

The benefit of this format for the musician is that, if you do heavily orchestrated stuff, it can handle mixing as many tracks as you can record. And if your trombone player is in Cleveland, you can shoot him what you've done on MDM, he does as many takes as he needs to, and shoots it to any similarly equipped studio, where it can be flown into the mix.

If you have some need to do an almost endless number of takes or to stack up sound like planes hovering over La Guardia, or if you've got a trombone player in Cleveland, you should probably consider MDM.

HARD DRIVE RECORDING

Digital hard drive recording is the future. Systems are expensive at the moment. The basic system has only two inputs, and top-of-the-line equipment of this sort—24-track digital hard drive—costs much more than comparable analog systems. Because these machines record at 600 megabytes per hour, the studio may have some very real concerns about the amount of storage space any single project may take up.

Your concern, as the recording artist, is limited to the all-too-familiar but nevertheless still frightening specter—the computer crash. Technology does fail, as engineers who are dedicated to analog are quick to point out. (Insert eerie ghostlike sounds here.)

Tape, on the other hand, is subject only to shredding, jamming, breaking, stretching, wow and flutter, leakage and other electronic distortions, drop-outs, emulsion breakdown, and oxide layers (all of which demand retakes, if not starting the entire project over). With analog tape, the closer you are to the end of the project, the more costly a tape screw-up may be. Compare that with computer crashes, which are "usually recoverable," and it gives you some idea about how very cool digital hard drive recording can be.

Digital hard drive recording involves no tape at all until the project is complete. You record directly into a computer audio board. And your work is backed up on an outboard backup system, so if there is a crash, you've still got a copy. The best feature is easy and versatile editing. Since you're actually recording right to the hard drive, when you've finished playing, the recording is already loaded for editing (so you've eliminated the real-time loading costs of other digital methods).

The sound is displayed on a monitor screen digitally in a visual wave pattern. You can hear it through speakers, and you can look at it on the screen. You have the ability to cut and paste on screen. Trim it, delete it, duplicate it. Data can be moved around readily and easily. So if, for example, you nailed a particular phrase in the first go-round and muffed it next time 'round, you can take the digital wave form that represents the good passage, copy it, and replace the muffed version. Without playing a note, you've fixed your flub. Suddenly your technique is flawless. The sound can be digitally faded, and instruments can be digitally doubled. The recording is mixed and sequenced and mastered all on screen. No tape is involved until you're satisfied. Then you make whatever copies you feel are needed on DAT.

Other good news: The recording is sampled at the same rate as CDs, so it can easily be mastered for CD.

MULTITRACKS

The point of using multiple tracks in any format is to achieve separation *and* to get as many takes as possible before mixing. Sound sources (instrument or voice) are typically isolated in order to ensure that they are recorded without any sound leakage from any other source. These isolated channels can then be given individual attention. Equalization (EQ) is established for each channel separately in order to enhance the desired tones as well as to eliminate unwanted tones. And individual sound levels are established in order to maintain clarity and to achieve a relative balance. Each of these factors allows for flexibility when "building" compositions (orchestration) in the mix.

With multiple tracks, orchestration is basically a matter of bringing one track to the surface while other tracks slip to various levels underneath. This is commonly done through adjusting levels, by ducking and keying, panning, and adjusting EQ.

Channels and Tracks

Lines in to the board, from mics or other input devices, are called channels. Each channel can feed its own separate track, or it can be premixed with other channels to be recorded together onto a given track. So six channels coming in does not necessarily mean you're using six tracks. It could. Or it could mean those six lines in are being recorded simultaneously to as few as one single track. Recording several channels simultaneously speeds up the overall recording process and keeps additional tracks open. But be cautious.

Once any two *channels* are mixed to the same *track*, they are permanently, inextricably mixed. There is nothing you can do to separate them again.

Here's a hypothetical example. Someone suggests that you can keep another track open by mixing the cymbals with the bass drum (something that has probably been done at one time or another). Well, OK. Sounds good. Why not? They're all drums anyway. They'll end up on the same track eventually.

- But then, in the final mix, when you decide that the cymbals should go left and the bass drum go right, it can't be done.

- If, at some point in the tune, the cymbals need to sit up on the surface while the bass slips underneath, that can't be done. The two are tied together. Where one goes, the other goes.

- If you want to get rid of the cymbals altogether, that can't be readily done without affecting the bass.

- If you need to tweak the EQ of the cymbals to get that perfect sound in the mix, you are at the same time screwing up the clarity of the bass drum.

That's why things are kept separate. And those are the kind of things you need to consider when determining how many tracks you might need. If you're absolutely sure you're *not* going to want to feature some particular channel in the mix, then there's no reason why it should not be premixed.

Tracks
Each *track* records one or more *channels*. That track is then kept separate in order to preserve its fidelity until it's ready to take its place in the mix. Each track can be recorded, recorded over, left out altogether, adjusted, processed, or erased, all without affecting the other tracks. That way, if you've got a killer vocal on one track but the guitar accompaniment is not yet up to snuff, you do not have to retake the vocal in order to retake the guitar. Or if you have several great guitar tracks, you can choose from among them and match the best one with the vocal. Or you can use all three guitar tracks with the vocal. Basically you can mix tracks together in any way you choose.

So How Many Tracks Do You Need?
Each instrument has its own particular micing requirements. A drum set, miced properly, may require three to six tracks by itself. A piano can take two. Acoustic guitars can take a couple each (it's not atypical to mic both the instrument and an amp to achieve a fatter or deeper sound). And you'll probably either want, or need, more than one take to choose from. Consider three to five shots at harmonies and as many for vocals and a couple for sweetener.

Even with all of this, some tracks will be needed for technical reasons, to mix to and to be used as reference tracks. It adds up pretty quickly, and the logic behind 24-track studios suddenly becomes clear. These days 24 tracks is the standard, but it's really a toss-up. The question remains, do *you* need 24 tracks?

Just because the current pop legend is recording on 48 tracks doesn't mean your results will be better because you fill up a lot of tracks with sound. In fact, unless your music demands many tracks (something heavily layered or with complex orchestration, for example), more tracks are as much of a burden as a benefit. The more tracks you fill up, the more difficult it becomes to decide precisely how they're going to mix down to two tracks. In any format too many choices only makes tracking, editing, and mixing more difficult. Too many choices can easily turn into a nightmare, especially your first time going in.

Alfonso X, king of Castile, comes to mind. After being introduced to Ptolemy's astronomical system, Alfonso said, "If the Lord Almighty had consulted me *before* embarking upon Creation, I should have recommended something simpler." The good king knew what he was talking about. Keep it simple so you can handle it.

There are budget considerations as well. Studios with smaller boards (fewer tracks) generally charge a lower fee. There are some *great* studios that have what some might consider lesser equipment. So don't waste good money on tracks you have no real use for. Determine how many tracks you need and avoid unnecessary complications.

Two-track is worth consideration for soloists, duos, and even larger ensemble groups working with a lot of (orchestrated) harmony. This is called live-mix to two-track. If the desired orchestration is accomplished during tracking and you have no need to do overdubbing, two tracks may be enough to capture that "live" sound.

If the price of an old 16-track joint will get you into the studio and give you a little ceiling on your budget, thus buying you a little extra time, then you should consider it. For a four- or five-piece unit looking for a nice raw, live sound, 16 tracks should be more than enough. Go in as a herd, set up, do the same song (same tempo) three times. You'll have a couple of tracks to fool around on and one to mix to. Three shots at the song, plus sweetener. You'll get a nice live sound.

If you go with 16-track, be understanding of what that might mean to the engineer. There are 16 tracks to work with, and the rhythm section may use up more than half of them laying down the bed tracks. That means you may have to bounce tracks (combine them) in order to continue tracking. And one of the points of multitracking is to have more takes from which to choose *before mixing*. Mixing is a different process and demands a different focus than tracking, so it's usually, purposefully, kept separate. Bouncing also disrupts the flow of the project.

Remember, however you record it, it all gets mixed down to two-track stereo.

ON THE OTHER HAND

Of course, you'll want to have as many options and as much control as you possibly can. Unless you have a clear vision as to the exact arrangement of each tune before going in, you may need to keep as much separate as you can, for as long as you can. Multitrack literally means separate tracks, which literally means options.

The first thing to decide is how many guitars, drums, voices, and so on actually require their own track. That determines how many tracks you may need. *If you're not sure,* you might want to keep as much as you can on separate tracks. If you're recording the rhythm parts to different tunes in one session, you might want to keep as much as you can on separate tracks (since the orchestration of each tune will be different).

The important question is, are there any key instruments (lead or solo or sweetener) that, for purposes of the arrangement, will need to separate themselves out from the rest? If so, each of these demands a separate track.

With all that good stuff each on separate tracks, it is more likely than not that you're going to need to make some room in order to continue tracking.

Freeing up Tracks

At any point during tracking, you can mix any of the existing tracks, thus freeing up additional tracks. But remember that *separation* is the reason you chose multitracking. When you start focusing on ways to free up tracks, it's easy to inadvertently lose sight of that point. In other words, both premixing channels and bouncing tracks will open up tracks, but they can also defeat your purpose. Once channels are premixed or tracks bounced, they are rendered (individually) unalterable. If you premix the piccolo with the fife, they can't be separated. And after you bounce the bass and then use that track to record vocals, there's virtually nothing you can do to separate the bass out again.

Bouncing

Mixing a track with a previously recorded track to another track is called bouncing. Bouncing should be carefully planned.

If you're satisfied with a take, and you're satisfied with the track it will be mixed with, there's no reason not to bounce it. But unless what's on each of those tracks is precisely what you want, do not bounce them. If it's not your best take or there are any problems with it at all, you'll only be mixing problems in with the good stuff. Every aspect of both tracks must be considered, especially sound levels. Make sure both tracks are free of any noise or unwanted sound. Also, one of the things you'll be bouncing in the analog format will be distortion. Every generation adds a little distortion. In short, don't sacrifice clarity and separation in order to free up tracks.

The only way to guarantee perfect acoustic separation is soloing—recording each instrument or voice in the studio by itself. In soloing, the only sounds on that track are the sounds of that particular instrument or voice. However, even sounds recorded this way can suffer problems. Noise can leak onto other tracks due to machine problems or problems with the tape itself (crosstalk).

If you have all the time in the world and a limitless bank account, this is the purest way to record your music. Overdubbing to previously recorded tracks by soloing each piece guarantees you the best possibly fidelity of sound. It's pretty much the way performers with the biggest budgets get that big-budget sound. The down side is that recording this way deprives you of all the factors that feed life into ensemble recording, so it may not result in the best representation of your music.

If you do not have all the time in the world and all the money too (let's say you have only one of these factors to play with), the usual solution is to track as much as you can premixed and reserve soloing for key instrumentals, vocals, and sweetener. This approach—tracking ensemble (live mix)—is the one most commonly used. It allows you to do more takes before going to the mix. The point of live mix is to go in, record as many pieces as possible all at once, and have it over with . . . just burn tape, as they say. Put the rhythm section or the horn section or the entire band in the studio and track them simultaneously. If you're aiming at spontaneity and that live feel, this is the way to go.

The main problem with recording this way is ensuring the isolation of each instrument in order to guarantee separation of the various sounds. A great deal of setup is required, both at the board and in the studio. At the board, establishing EQs and levels for each channel can become quite complex. In the studio, baffles and blankets and sometimes strange spur-of-the-moment inventions are put in place in an attempt to keep each microphone from picking up stray sounds from other instruments. Thus, success, when tracking ensemble is usually measured in degrees of acceptability.

Blues guitarist Nancy Dalessandro tells this somewhat instructive tale:

> When I was with the Rocket 88's out of Phoenix, we always recorded live. We didn't do any dry tracks and then go back in to overdub.
>
> This one time we'd already done all our tunes. We had everything down. So we were at the mixing stage and just listening back and trying to get the balance. And in one of the songs my guitar sounded really distorted. It just wasn't clean enough. We needed a better sound. So we decided to do the guitar over again. It was like a 24-bar solo. It had been totally improvised.
>
> I was gonna go right into the board, since I didn't have my amp set up anymore and they didn't want to go back and set up microphones. So we did that . . . took down the guitar track. But that's how we discovered that there was leakage from my track to all the other tracks. You could still hear the original solo coming through on each track. Like on the bass track, you could still hear it. So what were we gonna do? There was only one thing we could do. We decided that I had to redo the solo matching the original note for note.
>
> I had to go home and listen to the thing and relearn *my own solo*. I

worked on it for two days straight, trying to relearn my own solo—which was a pain in the butt. It was bad. It was torture. I went back in and went into the board with it and did the whole thing over again note for note. And when I heard the playback . . .

Well, we used it because the song was good, but it just sounded totally . . . . It was real stiff sounding, no passion, no spontaneity. And I'd worked on it for two days. I don't recommend doing that ever. It would have been better just to scrap it. That was just one of my nightmare experiences in the studio.

There's a point at which you should just give it up and maybe go back in a few days later or something, get a fresh start on it. Just make sure if you're recording live that you make good use of blankets and baffles so that there's good separation. That way, if you have to redo something, it doesn't leak onto other tracks and cause a problem.

The important question for you, in this typical studio horror story, is, at what point could this problem have been prevented? At what point should it have been detected and turned around? How could it have been stopped before it got to the artist having to spend days learning her own ad-lib fill? In short, what could the guitarist have done to prevent the problem? The answer: *routine.* Her solo should have been routine going in. There's a place for you to improvise stratospheric solos, but that place is not in the studio . . . at least not at this point.

Nancy Dalessandro's tale might also be a story about testing or about the importance of having an attentive producer on board. This leakage should have been detected early on, during tracking. After the first take, a request to hear each track separately is not unreasonable. It takes time, but it's worth it. Likewise, let the engineer take the time to look at things carefully. Wouldn't you rather have the engineer tell you, "Stand by, please," while locating this kind of problem and doing whatever is necessary to resolve it, than face what Dalessandro faced?

ONCE YOU'VE SETTLED ON A STUDIO

Once you've selected a studio, you've embarked on a journey. If your hopes are that this journey will lead you to a career working in the music industry, then I encourage you to start a sourcebook. Spend a few bucks and get yourself a nice notebook—something that's roadworthy and built to last. From this point on, enter the names and numbers of the people you come into contact with. If while looking for a studio, you met people who made some real sense to you, enter them into your sourcebook. Make a habit of listing everybody you come into contact with. Make notes on the circumstances under which you met so that when you call them you'll have a reference. Note what they do, whether they were helpful or not. Put the name in ink, spelled correctly and legibly, everything else in pencil. If they have a title, get the title right. Keep their business cards in a separate file.

After you've worked with people who make sense to you, even if you're not working together at the moment, call them once in a while. Stay in contact. The point of this contact is to find out what they are doing. Maybe you can make a connection for them with someone else you have in your sourcebook. That's the way the music business really works, on all levels.

If you come away with nothing more from this book, this suggestion alone should be worth the price. A good sourcebook will prove invaluable to you many times while on your journey.

Once you've selected a studio, supply your engineer with a tape of yourself or someone you like the sound of so that he or she can determine how that sound was recorded. Good studios will say thank you and take the time to listen. In the end, it makes their job easier to know what you have in mind; it will save time in the mix if the engineer knows what you're after during tracking. Before you arrive for your first session, the studio will be set up to achieve that effect.

Telling the engineer what kind of equipment you're planning to use will also help. Some engineers refer to this as instrumentation. "What kind of instrumentation are we talking about for the third session?" Answer: "The horn section. Couple of saxophones and a guy on kazoo."

GOOD ADVICE FROM THE ENGINEER

You may not want to hear it, but a good engineer will tell you that you can't get that $800,000 sound for $1,200; you can't get the purity of an L5 using some knock-off from Hong Kong; you can't get the unmuddled depth of double humbuckers using single-wound pickups; and a really crummy amp, properly miced and recorded perfectly, will sound exactly like what it is—a really crummy amp. The good engineer should give you good advice, and part of that means being honest with you while explaining the trade-offs.

Don't confuse something you do not want to hear with bad advice. The best advice musicians are offered is *almost always something they do not want to hear*. The mistake is to reject such advice out of hand.

If the studio recommends that you use their equipment, that's not a sign they're trying to milk you. It's probably a very good indicator that they have your best interests in mind. Engineers are not concerned about your money so much as they are about sound quality. The recommendation that you use in-house equipment is usually a good one. The instruments are superior. They're professionally set up, tuned, and will render a better sound. The staff is familiar with this equipment and they know how best to set it up, mic it, and establish its EQ. All of which adds up to better results for you. It's worth asking the price.

Try to convince the engineer to come hear you play live. See where that goes. Explain that he or she doesn't have to stay through the entire blistering set but maybe just a couple of tunes. This is a special request on your part, but by catching your act, the engineer will have a better idea, going in, of what you're after and how to capture it on tape. Also, by seeing you play live, he or she will be able to forewarn you about anything you're doing on stage that you can't get away with in the studio. Both of these things will make the engineer's job easier and the project go more smoothly. Such insight is especially important if you're going to be asking this person to take on the added role of producer.

If the engineer actually shows up at the gig, "give 'em" the royal treatment: comped in, good seats, and cold beer. If he's a guy, prop some blonde beside him with instructions to giggle at everything he says. If the engineer is a woman, substitute some guy with a French accent for the blonde. This is standard procedure, steeped in tradition. And don't forget to pack the house with friends and shills. It can't hurt to give the impression that you've got a following. If the engineer thinks people are actually going to hear the results of his or her work, your project may receive a little extra consideration.

After you're booked, if there's any time left before going in, hammer out a schedule, appoint a producer, check out your equipment, consolidate your repertoire, and finalize the routine of each tune you plan to record. From that point on, it's rehearse, rehearse, rehearse.

Charlie Musselwhite advises:

> Be as prepared as possible. It costs a lot of money to be in the studio, you know . . . the tape and the musicians, the engineers, and rental of the studio. Plus, if it's a popular studio, when your time is up, there's another group coming in right then. So if something's gone wrong, you can't stay and fix it. You've gotta get out of there. Usually that's the way it is. Some people just lock out a studio for days at a time or even months. But most people, especially people starting out, should have rehearsed all their tunes so well that all they have to do is go in, get set up, get the tones and everything like they want them, get everything miced right, and just cut it. No dilly-dallying around. . . . Of course, there's gotta be a certain amount of dilly-dallying around, just to get comfortable with the environment and the people you work with, the engineers and stuff, so that you feel relaxed. You don't want to feel like you're watching the clock, but in the back of your mind, you should realize that this is business.

3

STUDIO PERSONNEL

T HE RECORDING STUDIO PROFESSIONALS
you deal with will do everything they can to give you the best possible results.
Although they may not be invested in your career, they *are* invested inextricably
in your tape. It represents the kind of work they are capable of to everyone who
hears it. If you recognize that fact, if you recognize that you and the recording
studio staff are a team, it can lead to a better working situation and, consequently, better results.

Many upstart musicians think that if the results of their studio work are not
what they expected, it's the engineer's fault, but if the results are great, it can
only be attributed to their own brilliant musicianship. Actually, the exact opposite is probably the case. A good engineer can make a mediocre musician sound
pretty damned good, but even the best engineer cannot perform miracles. If the
results are terrible, it's most likely because there was not enough for the engineer to work with. If the results are great, they could not have gotten that way
without a good engineer at the board.

Of course, what's good and what's not are a matter of perspective. The engineer's job has been done well, however, if the sounds created in the studio are
recorded with clarity and depth. Even the most horrendous musical embarrassment can be recorded with all the necessary considerations to produce a good
mix. The fact that the music remains lousy has nothing to do with the engineer.
"Gee, Bill, you really did a great job of capturing just how weary, stale, flat, and
unprofitable that hired horn player turned out to be."

A major factor in getting results that are good in your own eyes and in the
engineer's as well is communication. During the project the person who does the
major share of communication with the studio staff is the producer.

THE PRODUCER

A lot of studio time is wasted by first-timers because they go in thinking that recording is some kind of democratic, utopian, or egalitarian experiment. It is not. When it comes to decisions in the studio, whether it's during a tracking session or in the mix, you need *one* person, and one only, in the booth to represent your needs. To have more than one person in there, unless others are specifically asked in, is costly, time-consuming, and unprofessional. It's usually confusing and counterproductive as well.

That one person in the booth is your producer. Typically, the producer handles everything from studio selection to final master approval and all the steps in between. Generally, he or she oversees all aspects of the project from beginning to end. In the studio, it's the producer who communicates your needs to the engineer, maintains all communications with the studio, and sees that all bills are paid on time. Outside, the producer oversees preproduction and postproduction.

In the beginning, the producer may help you select a studio, decide between digital and analog, schedule studio time and rehearsals. The producer is there to help you decide which tunes to record, how best to record them, and even the order in which you'll record them. The producer may have a hand in arrangement and orchestration of your work and may accept responsibility for obtaining necessary mechanical rights and securing the rights to your songs. If necessary, the producer will probably purchase tape and equipment. He or she will see that you get there when you're supposed to be there and that you're not there when you're not needed. Not all babysitters are producers, but all producers are babysitters of a sort. It's certainly one aspect of the job.

The producer is liaison between the artist and the studio—your voice in the booth. If what goes on in the booth between the engineer and the producer is a combination of art and science, the producer takes the aesthetic view. During the session the producer sits at the board with the engineer, but it is *not* the producer's job to oversee the technical aspects of recording or to offer the engineer advice. Even good advice, no matter how diplomatically offered, will probably cause more harm than good.

The producer *is* there, however, to see that the engineer handles everything in the manner necessary to best attain what you, the musician, may want. He or she is there to see that you get enough takes to use in the mix, to make sure that important details are noted, to look after your best interests. Master of logistics, the producer maintains both the short and the long view of the entire project.

During the session, the producer is the person you ask if you'd like to hear a playback.

In the end, the producer oversees the mix. He or she participates in editing, helps select and sequence your tunes, establishes playing times, decides which tunes to "pass" on and which tunes to leave in. The producer makes sure your master has variety—differing tempos, moods, styles, keys—and oversees mastering and approval of the final mix. And if things work out as in some kind of fairy tale, the producer may be in the position to offer your tape to a label. Or it may work the other way around; your tape could be such a fine example of the producer's abilities that it becomes his or her connection to a label. So it benefits both of you for the producer to do the best job possible. That's why you can trust your producer.

A common mistake for first-timers is to spend so much time laying down basic tracks—tracks that will, more likely than not, be buried in orchestration or masked by sweetener—that they inadvertently put themselves in a time crunch. Consequently, key instrumental tracks and vocals are squeezed in up against the clock, when everybody is worn out. It's the producer's job to see that this doesn't happen. It's the producer's job to see that you have enough studio time to record the vocals and work on polishing the thing up a bit with harmony and instrumental sweeteners. Whatever time you've spent laying perfect bed tracks is wasted if what's on the surface is rushed.

Naturally, all musicians want to record their very best efforts. They want to do their piece over again (and over again and over again), until they've either gotten it perfect or have driven everyone stark raving mad in the attempt. This is the point at which a little contention may arise. But don't get angry if the producer says it's time to move on. Getting emotionally involved is probably necessary to the task of doing your best work in the studio, but anger doesn't accomplish anything. If the producer says it's time to move on, then it's probably time to move on.

It's the producer's job to ride herd on sticking to the project schedule. The producer has the authority to ask you to try another take, to say when a take is satisfactory, to insist that you move on, to suggest that everybody take a break, or to stop the session altogether and send everybody home. Of course, you have to keep working on the project until it's complete, and every part needs to be right, but studio time is expensive and it needs to be managed. That's the producer's role.

WHEN TO QUIT

Knowing when to stop is important, but the musician is usually too close to the project to recognize it when that time arises. Even professionals have a difficult time knowing when they've reached that point. Usually it takes someone else to point it out. The producer's motto is, don't push it if it isn't working.

It's perfectly understandable why someone performing solo in an empty room for the first time might have some difficulty. The experience is probably unlike anything the artist has ever experienced before. It's not unusual for things to bog down a bit. When things are going so badly that the producer thinks maybe you should just wrap it up, then maybe you should. If it's not working, go home. Come back another day and give it another shot.

Patrick Ford tells this story about some of the finest musicians around not knowing when to quit:

I remember when Robben Ford was cutting *The Inside Story* album. This was a monster four-piece band and this was their first recording together. My family and I just dropped in to check out the session while we were in L.A. They were doing this really cool instrumental that Robben had written. When we got there, they were like on take seven, but they weren't really happy with it. By take 16 or 17, some of which were complete takes and some of which weren't, they hit a take I thought was great. And when they came into the booth to listen to it, I said to Robben, "That's a *great* take, man. You should save it. You guys are going to start getting into the tired zone here pretty quick. I'm telling you, this is a great take!"

Well, three of the guys liked it but the bass player said, "I can do better than that." So they all trudged back into the studio. And, you know, on take 32 we left. And that song never made it onto the album. So the ego of each musician has to be controlled in one way or another. Either the artist has to do it himself—which is very tough—or they have to get some other ears to lean on.

First time in, of course, you probably won't have the luxury of walking away just because things aren't working out perfectly. So take a break. There's no sense in continuing if you're just bending nails, making bad cuts, and burning up expensive saw blades. After the break, if it's still not working, change things around a bit by going off schedule. Give yourself a chance. But if the problems continue, the producer may insist that you quit. That's the producer's call. Arguing about such stuff is a true waste of everybody's time.

First-timers sometimes associate the need to wrap things up early with failure. But if you've gone as far as you can for the day, there's no stigma attached to closing the session. If things are just flying apart at the seams, it's the wise thing to do. You do not want to come away from the studio feeling like you've had an irreparable experience. Playback can be an excellent wrapping tool.

Dick Shurman, who has produced artists like Johnny Winter, Roy Buchanan, Albert Collins, Otis Rush, Charlie Musselwhite, and Johnny Heartsman, offers this advice:

> Don't ever think that you can guarantee that the session is going to be hot or go smoothly. All you can do is to hope to minimize the failure points, cross your fingers, and maximize the controllable circumstances. When working with certain people, I discovered that all we had to do to make a session go hard was to say, "This should be easy." On the other hand, to make things go easy, all we had to do was say, "Well this is probably going to take a while, but we're just gonna have to dig in and do it." Do everything you can to put yourself in a position to succeed, but realize that that's not the way life works, either in the studio or out of it.

Another important part of the producer's job is to offer encouragement and keep a little fun in the project. Jeff Forrest (Doubletime Studios, San Diego) says:

"As a musician, I know there's nothing worse than having a technician just rolling tape and being cold to your needs. So the very first thing you do when they come in is make them feel really happy. Real happy and real at ease. Anything to get them loosened up and to have fun. Make them feel totally at ease so that they feel like they're just rehearsing. That way, by the time you start rolling tape, they don't even know tape is rolling. I do that so their performance comes out better. That's a big part of my job."

Psychologist-turned-producer Blair Hardman (Zone Recording, Cotati, California) tells me that when things get too tense in the studio, he secretly switches on a harmonizer so that all the whining comes back through the cans sounding like Alvin and the Chipmunks. He says that usually puts things in a more reasonable perspective.

THE PRODUCER'S ASSOCIATION WITH THE STUDIO

Throughout the project it's the producer who maintains all contact with the studio. Only the producer. Every working musician knows first-hand what kind of problems can develop when more than one person makes contact with someone you're working with. To have more than one person making arrangements is unprofessional and is almost guaranteed to lead to trouble.

Before each session the producer should confer with the engineer and confirm what you intend to do in the studio during the coming session. The engineer needs to know what instruments are being used and how they're going to be recorded. The studio needs to be informed of any changes that may crop up concerning your schedule. If, according to the schedule, you're ready to do vocals that day and you've decided instead to let the guitar player overdub his part, it can lead to a considerable loss in time while the engineer makes readjustments and the technician sets up the room for this unexpected change of events.

After each session, before leaving the studio, the producer should check the log to be sure it has all the settings—EQ, mics used, studio arrangement, gain on the pre-amps, and so forth—so that the engineer can dial in quickly during the setup of subsequent sessions. The producer is not there to tell the engineer what to do, but keeping the project on schedule entails anticipating the next move and quietly overseeing the preparation of others.

If this is a commercial project, generally the producer gets royalties (an agreed-upon percentage of all units sold). So if you're planning to sell the results of your studio work, you need to decide how your producer is going to be paid. For signed artists, royalties are paid only after recouping costs, but producers are paid from unit one. Some producers will work for a flat fee. If you can get away with a flat fee, swing that deal. Producer's royalties are a key factor when artists find themselves *losing* money on every unit sold.

While working with the producer, as with all studio personnel—if you have any questions or doubts about what's going on—ask. If you have needs, express them. Your role in relation to the producer can be either pawn or dictator. Chicago wisdom suggests that you either control completely or completely surrender control. Anything in between only muddies the waters. And whatever your position, make it clear.

At this stage in the game, you should probably give up control while in the studio. Continually check to assure yourself that things are understood, of course, and heading in the right direction. Take the time between sessions to review what's going on. If the producer needs further instruction, provide it before returning for the next session, but do not waste studio time arguing.

FINDING A PRODUCER

Finding a real producer can be difficult enough. Finding the right producer may be an impossible task. Producers are somewhat like drummers—a good one is hard to find and a bad one is hard to get rid of. Hard to get rid of because, once you're submersed in a project, you're pretty much locked in until it reaches some conclusion, successful, catastrophic, or otherwise. So selecting a producer is an important decision.

Producers can be hired guns or someone from your band who has never produced before (a pseudo producer). And occasionally the difference between the two may be, in actuality, negligible. On the other hand, the difference could also be both enormous and critical. There are certainly good producers and bad producers. A producer who is excellent producing one type of music may prove ineffectual producing something different.

Many people pass themselves off as producers. For example, 27 people claimed the title "Producer" and advertised themselves as such in a little local music directory published several years ago in San Diego. According to their listings, they did everything: arrangement, production, manufacturing, consultation, promotion. Some of them had produced "film scores for award-winning, internationally distributed productions." They offered to "turn your dream into reality." Naturally, many of them insisted on dealing with "professionals only." Remember, though, that anyone can have a business card made. Anyone can pay a fee to be listed in a music directory.

But there's a divinity that shapes our ends, rough-hew them as we will, and two years down the road, only four of those producers are still around. If your guess is that the other 23 all turned their own dreams into reality and moved to L.A., you might want to guess again. In the interim—until they discovered for themselves that they weren't really cut out to be producers—hopeful artists were paying them good money to produce their work.

A GENERAL WORD OF CAUTION

In the music biz people claim to be all kinds of things. Some guy who saw Bob Dylan emerge from the Whitehorse Tavern on Bleecker Street one morning now claims to be his close personal friend. A bass player who played a gig on the same night, same city, as Muddy Waters claims to have toured with him. Some guy who wrote a letter to Cher and never got a response claims to have turned down the opportunity to manage her career. Talk to anyone who has ever bought a used LP at a garage sale and, given the chance, they'll yammer on for 20 minutes about their direct, inside industry connections.

When you start looking at producers, begin with their track records. Look at the stuff they've produced before. Ask to see *physical evidence* of work they've done—CDs with their name listed as producer are always nice. If, unfortunately, all evidence of someone's illustrious career was destroyed in the Malibu fire, then you might want to reconsider. A legit producer should be able to offer tangible evidence of previous work.

Once you've narrowed your search to a few legit producers, forget their reputations. The important questions now are, Which of them has produced work that makes sense to *you*? Which of them has an understanding of what *you're* trying to accomplish?

The good producer will always ask you what *you* think before telling you what he or she thinks. The producer's job is to accomplish what you're after.

Dick Shurman says, "I usually go in to the artist and say, 'Here's my deal: I promise to try it your way first if you'll promise to be open-minded about what I have to say about it.'" That's the kind of reasonable approach you're looking for.

The good producer may seem slow at times. There's a certain pace to the studio—and anytime the ball is in the producer's court, it can take some time before the return. The best producers, at times, also seem to be the slowest, because they take the time to really listen to things. They become absorbed in the task. They may listen to something several times before offering a suggestion. They may listen several times and reach no conclusion at all. Listening takes time. Listening is what you're paying the producer to do.

If your choice is between someone you're not sure of and someone you know, trust, and can speak to, go with the latter. If you can find somebody who actually understands the musical idiom you're working in, it makes a big difference. You want somebody who understands the music, somebody who can listen, somebody who can communicate your ideas to others. The person who understands what you're up to but can't convey it won't be much help to you in the booth.

If you're going to appoint a pseudo producer—someone you know but who has never produced before—make sure he or she knows what you're after. You have to feel confident that your needs are understood if you're going to agree to go by this person's decisions. That means, before going into the studio, you have to take the time to sit down and instruct your producer as to what you want and how you'd like to go about achieving it. Better yet, ask your producer to explain it to you. If the explanation isn't clear to you, it won't be any clearer in the booth.

Also make sure the pseudo producer understands the demands of the role of producer. (Make this chapter required reading.) If you have any doubts beforehand, be prepared to choose another candidate. If what goes down in the studio turns out to be disastrous, rather than have the project grind to a halt, have someone in mind to replace your pseudo producer.

Choose anybody other than yourself. An all-too-common mistake artists make is attempting to produce their own work. The producer has a separate task that requires a distancing from the music that most artists are incapable of, especially while tracking. Suffice it to say that professional recording artists who produce their own work are practically nonexistent (although many have a hand in the task). The few who do so successfully are recognized by people in the industry as monumental geniuses.

Take a lesson from military history. When General Militates beat the Greeks at Marathon, even though he knew the guy who delivered the good news would become a national hero (and live free of taxes for the rest of his life), he didn't try to run the 26 miles 385 yards himself. He appointed Philippides, a runner, to the task. This is a good studio strategy as well. Get the right person to handle each task, then allow them to do their jobs.

However you go about getting a producer in place, what's important for you is that you have someone in the booth to represent your wishes to the engineer. If you do not hire a professional, it's important that you do appoint *somebody* if any work is to get done.

Since the producer is there to convey what the artist has in mind and suggest possible answers to the engineer, finding a producer who has already worked with your engineer is a good idea. So the engineer is a good place to start asking about producers. You want people who can work together and can understand each other.

Dick Shurman relates this example of the kind of confusion that can arise otherwise.

There was one time when I was recording an acoustic tune with Johnny Winter. He was out in this big studio and it had a hardwood floor. And Johnny started tapping his foot on the floor, which was what John Lee Hooker used to do—they used to put a piece of plywood under his foot and mic it. So I heard Johnny's foot tapping and I said to the engineer, "Listen to that. We should do something about it." The engineer said, "OK, we'll do something." He called the second over to go get a piece of carpet to mute it. He thought I was trying to get it out of there. I wanted to capture it.

With that kind of confusion over a simple matter of micing or muting, what kind of results can you expect on the overall project?

The producer has to be part psychologist, part diplomat, sometimes part comedian. That person has to know how to relieve the tension and how to make suggestions without hurting anyone's feelings. It's the producer's job to help the artist overcome performance anxiety in the studio, to keep things moving on schedule and to re-instill the fun when things start to fall apart. When the playback is so damned bad you feel like you should just stop right then and put a loaded gun to your head, it's the producer's job to speak soothingly while gently peeling your finger from the trigger and get the project back on track.

The job of the producer is to make sure that things are under control. The producer has to have the ability to take in the big picture while keeping an eye on the details. Seemingly little things—like having enough tape—are actually critical, and the producer needs to recognize it. The producer has to know how to motivate people, to induce cooperation, and to offer comfort. It has to be someone who can generate confidence and be decisive without being autocratic. The producer has to be a person you can look to and know a decision is going to be made. So the ability to reach decisions is a good thing to look for in a producer.

Before the first session, make sure the ground rules are in place. *Everybody* must agree to respect the producer's decisions. If something happens in one of the sessions that you disagree with, wait until a break or ask for a break to talk it over. Don't take up studio time squabbling. If possible, wait until after the session. Give the producer a chance to explain the decisions you disagree with, but also be prepared to make heads roll if it becomes necessary. Whether you hire a producer or appoint one of your own, it's worth whatever time it takes to get someone in place whom you'll respect.

ENGINEER AS PRODUCER

Musicians going into the studio for the first time often expect the engineer to double as producer. Although that's a common expectation, it is not the engineer's job to be your producer. It's not the best idea either, because the engineer's role is demanding and requires a different focus, as well as ongoing attention. What you're really doing, when you ask the engineer to produce, is asking them to divide their attention.

Nonetheless, if you do not have a producer or can't find one, you may need to depend on the engineer. You cannot expect yourself to keep track of the overall project, tend to the details, work with the engineer, and perform all at the same time. If you can see the complete ball game while you're wrapped up in your own work, then you're not wrapped up tightly enough in your own work.

To ask the engineer to also serve as producer is a special request. If that is your hope, however, *ask*. Demonstrate some appreciation if the answer is yes. Don't be surprised if the rate escalates according to the added role, however. Again, engineer and producer are two separate tasks.

THE RECORDING ENGINEER

The engineer's job is to record every track with consideration for the ultimate desired mix. The goal is to capture all of the sounds made in the studio with optimal fidelity in order, ultimately, to obtain the best possible representative master. Generally this entails establishing the perfect EQ on each line in, so that the greatest clarity is achieved, and getting as much gain as possible with the least amount of distortion on each track. The engineer looks toward the greatest dynamic range, optimizing the signal-to-noise ratio and trying to attaining the best over-all frequency response. If there's a high up there so high that only dogs can hear it, the engineer's job is to capture it cleanly if it's important to your music.

Engineers monitor their own success or failure electronically, quantitatively, through the board. That's what all that expensive equipment is about. Generally they know when they're accomplishing their task. Quantifiable parameters of any sort are their business. So you do not need to concern yourself with things like bandwidth, dispersion, filters, gate and peak limitations, hard knee, the noise floor, phantom power, power handling, secondary reflective sound, signal-to-noise ratios, soft knee, tonal nuance, total harmonic distortion, track, and machine offsets. All of these are the engineer's concerns.

What you need to keep in mind is that recording is *the engineer's* business. In the studio *your* business is to play. If some sort of difficulty comes up concerning the engineer, inform the producer and let those two work it out.

Undoubtedly there are some engineers who are better than others and some you might work with more easily. Few are actually outright incompetent. The nature of the craft is so meticulous and so demanding that only certain analytical types are attracted to the job to begin with and those who are not built for it are weeded out pretty quickly. That's one reason there is always so much really neat, virtually unused, high-end home recording equipment for sale in the paper. People buy the stuff thinking it will be fun but find out pretty quickly how demanding sound engineering can be, even on the amateur level.

A bad engineer, then, is not necessarily someone who can't run the electronics well but someone who may have no feel for, or understanding of, your music.

If you've got yourself a slimy little four-piece thrash unit grinding out ear-shattering, chunky rhythms under some skinny little psychotic chick in tights screeching about vomiting at the top of her lungs, and your engineer wants to do anything more than put you in there as a herd, mic you four ways, and go right to two-track with it, then maybe you should reconsider. On the other hand, some of the finest string ensemble recordings have been accomplished with one mic (or a stereo array) hanging down into the sweet-spot from a beam of an old church ceiling. It's the engineer's sensitivity to the music that leads to the recording method that makes the most sense.

The point is this: no matter how great as a technician, an engineer who has no real feel for your music is of no use to you. The very best producer can't be expected to overcome such an obstacle. An engineer who doesn't understand or care about your music will be helpless to capture it on tape. Just as the engineer can't be expected to fully educate you about the recording process, you shouldn't have to teach the engineer an appreciation for your music.

Engineer is a vital position and crucial to the success of your project. Once you've found the right one, trust him or her. Engineers know about things like the Haas effect, harmonics and subharmonics, overtones and subtones, direct, reflective, and secondary reflective sound. In their minds, the audio band spectrum is divided into a dozen or more distinct zones, and they don't need a chart to keep track of it. Good engineers deserve respect for their knowledge.

Nevertheless, if the engineer says, "Don't worry, we'll fix that in the mix," you might ask for a clarification. Some engineers, we're told, use that phrase to cover technical mistakes in the hope of putting off the problem. The hope is to avoid wasting time tinkering with something that will eventually be scrapped. What the engineer might really be saying is "We'll fix it in the mix *if* it makes it to the mix." Or there may be another explanation. Either way, the engineer may be trying to alleviate frustration and save a little time. If you think the explanation is plausible, accept it and move on.

Unless the producer speaks up, how much tape is used is up to the engineer. Some engineers save everything that goes down in a session. Some back up the tape at every opportunity and record over what they feel are bad or unusable takes. It's pretty much their call. They know what's needed for the mix and that's what they focus on. Unless told otherwise, the engineer's job is only to save what might be usable and needed. Make your wants clear to your producer before the session or, if there's any doubt, before the next take is slated. If you think part of the take you just did is worth saving, say so.

Here's Charlie Musselwhite:

On one of my albums with Alligator, there's a tune called "Catwalk," which was just a tune we were foolin' around with in the studio. I didn't go into the studio with that tune in mind. It was just a warmup instrumental, but it had this nice sound to it and I said, "Let's just cut this thang!" And that's what we did. It wasn't the greatest tune ever recorded in the history of music, but it was a nice little tune. That kind of unexpected thing happens. And if you're in the studio when that happens, it can be a tune.

It's been said that Frank Zappa *always* had the tape rolling. Whether he was just noodling around or working on a major project, everything was captured on tape. Nothing was ever scrapped. That way, every bit of brilliance captured could be worked on and incorporated into later compositions. His compositions are replete with the reworkings of such outtakes. You might consider that.

The engineer may, at any time, stop taping if a technical problem demands it. If, despite efforts to save the take, the engineer is convinced that the take is ruined, it's lost. He or she knows what's usable and what's not. *If* such a thing occurs in the midst of what you feel is an especially hot take, the professional thing to do is . . . live with it. In most cases the engineer didn't cause the problem but only detected its presence. The appropriate response, after a 20-minute delay between takes, is to say thanks.

FINDING AN ENGINEER

Since most studios employ engineers—their wage is typically worked in as part of the studio rate—selection of the engineer might be limited by the studio you choose. The engineer is paid either as part of the studio fee or as a separate per hour rate. Be sure you're clear on which arrangement you have.

If you go looking for an engineer, the same rules apply as when looking for a producer. You want someone you can work with and someone who understands your music.

Charlie Musselwhite offers this advice:

> A good sound engineer is somebody who really knows the music. Especially, if you can, you want somebody who's a fan. That would be helpful because they'll be familiar with the music and be really excited to be a part of the project. That's the best of all worlds, somebody who knows you, who knows the music; somebody who's excited to be part of the project and is good at the job too.
>
> You can get someone who's a great engineer technically, but if that person doesn't understand the music, it can really get messed up. It'll come out flat and dead . . . where there's supposed to be life there won't be any. It'll be a great technical reproduction on one level, but the engineer will miss the point on feeling. And feeling is in the tones. That's where the feeling lies in records. An engineer who isn't sympathetic to the tones isn't going to capture the feeling.

Naturally, you want the best person you can get. But that doesn't necessarily mean the biggest person you can get. If, when you meet, the engineer is busy doing other things and aggressively denying you eye contact, maybe that person is too big to give your music the attention it deserves. Find someone you can work with, someone who at least pretends to want to work with you.

Dale Miller advises that when talking to potential engineers, "you want them to take you seriously. If the guy's just bored with you, to hell with him. I mean that's happened to me. He's eating a sandwich or he's looking at his watch; he just doesn't have time for you because you're not Bob Dylan or something. Well, that's just crap. You shouldn't put up with that."

Each engineer has a past. The question is, how well does the engineer's portfolio mesh with your work? Patrick Ford cautions:

> It's all in relation to the studio you're going to use. You can listen to a project an engineer did in one studio and think, "Hey, this guy is great." But that guy may work in that studio all the time; he knows that room. If you hire him and bring him to another studio, where he doesn't know the room, he doesn't know the board—yeah, he's competent—but he may waste a lot of time trying to figure out the tricks of that particular room. And he may never get you the sound that you heard on that record. So you want to listen to stuff that an engineer has done in the studio you're gonna work in. Or listen to stuff that he's done in a bunch of different studios, so you know he can handle a lot of different environments. If he hasn't worked in your

studio, that doesn't mean he can't handle it, but you may want to think about that.

The better informed the engineer is about what you're after, the better decisions that person can make in terms of helping you to achieve it. If you provide some tapes of other people's stuff that you are impressed with, the engineer may be able to tell you how they achieved that effect, what mics were used, how it was recorded, and so forth. For the sake of your project, you might feel more comfortable with someone who claims to have such insight.

On the other hand, it's no sign of inadequacy if the engineer can't promise you that same sound—things are pretty complex these days. Some musicians have developed unique approaches to playing that may be impossible to figure out. Guitar player Lafayette "The Thing" Thomas used his pinky on the knobs to get a continually changing tone that people who'd seen him play couldn't duplicate. With or without all the electronic wee-wah, Roscoe Beck can make a six-stringed bass sound like an organ. An engineer who has never seen these musicians, only heard them, might be unable to decipher such sounds.

The other side of that coin is, if you're going to ask someone to try to get a certain sound for you, *you* had better be able to deliver too.

Apparently George Harrison did this incredible solo on the Beatles' song "And Your Bird Can Sing." It had every guitarist in the world spraining finger tendons and wearing out hi-fi needles trying to duplicate it. But nobody could. Nobody. Every serious guitar player made the attempt.

Joe Walsh was just one of the ga-zillion guitar players out there trying to crack the code. After working on it for months, he did something no one else had done—he got to where he could play that thang note for note. Naturally, Joe was wise enough to feature the piece on stage, and word of it spread like wildfire in the guitar playing world. His shows were all packed, the audience consisting mainly of guitar players eager to see someone do what they personally knew to be impossible.

A thousand years later Joe was at a party in L.A. and bumped into Harrison. "Man, you are a great guitar player!" declared Walsh. "I mean, you are a great, great guitar player. It took me like a year and a half to nail that solo on 'And Your Bird Can Sing.' How did you ever come up with that?"

George Harrison looked at Joe Walsh and said, "It was double-tracked."

At that very moment Joe Walsh realized that he was the only person on the planet who could play that solo.

So just because a sound is on a record doesn't mean it got there naturally.

4

······························

THE LEXICON

······························

THIS CHAPTER OFFERS a lexicon of working terms. It is not a glossary. It is not just a bunch of words relegated to the back of the book for you to look up at your leisure. These are terms that you should probably know and understand in order to get along in the studio. With the right words you can establish a rapport, which can be vital to achieving the best outcome.

The essential point of studio jargon, or terminology, is communication. The more specifically you can articulate what you want, the better chance you have of getting it from both the engineer and your producer. On the other hand, it's difficult to verbalize music, and each artist has his or her own personal vocabulary. That's why tape is an excellent way to communicate what you want without using any words at all.

Charlie Musselwhite:

> I don't think it hurts to know as much as possible; we're talking about communication, you know. That's why I used the tape recorder sometimes. If I wanted to describe a tone . . . how can you, in words, describe a tone? You could say, "Well, it's kind of a hard tone" or "It's kind of a soft tone." But if you've got that sound on a tape, it's like a picture—worth a thousand words. When it comes to the kind of mics and micing techniques and stuff like that, you don't have to know all that, but it sure helps to know. I mean, actors know about lighting and stuff. If you're on the set, they'll say, "I'd like this light moved over here" or "I want this camera angle changed." They don't just walk through their parts; they know about all the things that affect their acting too. I don't think too much knowledge can hurt you.

The best sort of knowledge—meaning knowledge that pertains to your music—comes from being in the studio. You don't read it in a book. It's a matter of experience. Somewhere along the line you learn that if you hang a mic a certain way, in a certain position, you get the sound you want. Maybe you've sat in at other sessions and seen how other people do something or you've talked to another musician about how he or she accomplishes a particular sound. First time in, just keep your eyes and ears open.

THE IMPORTANCE OF TERMINOLOGY

Confusion can occur in the studio simply as part of the process. You can expect it. The views held by the musician and studio personnel can be, and usually are, distinctly, even radically different. Such differences are found at every level throughout the entire recording process. In addition, solutions to problems in the studio sometimes seem illogical from the musician's view.

Two examples of such differences should suffice.

To the musician, *outboard equipment* consists of devices for creating sound effects. To the engineer, however, any signal processing device, whatever its supposed aesthetic contribution, is yet another factor in an already demanding list of factors that must be monitored and quantitatively controlled in order to get the desired results, not now, but somewhere down the line, in the final mix.

Many musicians think that in order to capture that *deep bass sound,* you simply add lots of low end. Bass players seem to be especially convinced of this. But the engineer knows that the mid and high frequencies of the low instruments give them definition; to get the best sound out of a bass you have to EQ in some midrange. Though this be madness, yet there is method in it.

Separate views can lead to problems, but many arguments in the studio are merely a matter of semantics. An excellent example is the word *hot*. In blues and all its permutations (jazz, jump, swing, boogie, rock 'n' roll), *hot* means pushing or playing ahead of the beat. Playing behind the beat is *cool*. That's a musician's perspective. To the recording engineer, however, *hot* is capturing as much signal as possible. With analog, generally the louder the thing is recorded (without distortion), and the faster the tape is rolling, the hotter the recording. When the tape is saturated with as much information as possible, it's hot.

In digital recording (to the mastering engineer), *hot* takes on yet another meaning. It's something to be avoided. If things get hot, it means the sound is getting muddled, or worse, "crunchy." So depending on whom you're talking to and what format you're talking about, a simple word like *hot* can convey a peculiar variety of messages.

With that kind of confusion surrounding a frequently used word like *hot,* what is the engineer supposed to make of it when the artist says, "I want a little warmer sound"? Does that mean using a tube mic pre-amp or putting the artist in a livelier room or maybe using a carpeted room and adjusting the EQ to capture more mid-range? Would enhancing the lows do it? Can that warmer sound be gotten through reverb or through overdubbing? Could it be merely a matter of adjusting what the artist hears in his headphones? The solution to such requests sometimes goes against all logic.

Other questions also arise from such requests. Does this warmth thing need to be addressed now while tracking, or can it be tweaked in the mix? Adjustments made to achieve warmth may not even be evident at this point in the process. Perhaps warmth will surface when this track is mixed with other tracks later. Does the artist understand the implications if it's achieved now? On top of all that, how warm does the artist want it?

It's for the engineer, with guidance from the producer, to interpret such instructions and to make appropriate adjustment in how the signal is captured and recorded. Though there are almost standard responses for requests for fatter, heavier, thinner, warmer—is the usual solution the one that's best for your music? What's most important, in all of this, is for you to get your point across.

Dick Shurman tells us:

> Gatemouth Brown has a power chord thing that he calls a shock wave. *If you know what that is* and he tells you that's what he wants, then you can give it to him. Or he's got this other thing where he does a gliss and he calls it a "forward whip." Sometimes when he only goes halfway up with it, it's called a "half whip."

Obviously these aren't standard technological terms used by recording engineers throughout the industry. If you say you're gonna do a half-whip in the second bar, your engineer might not know how to respond. But as long as you can explain what you want in a way that the person at the board *can* understand, that's all you need. For you, as an artist, an equally important aspect of terminology is to understand what the studio professionals are trying to convey to you.

HOW MUCH DO YOU NEED TO KNOW?

In establishing a lexicon for the first-time artist, the real question arises, how much does the artist need to know? When engineers and producers are asked this question, the answers come back ranging from "They need to know as much as they possibly can" to "The more they know, the more they hang out in the booth and get in the way." An answer that seems to make sense is "They need to know enough to be comfortable and confident that they'll be getting the results they want."

It's important to keep in mind why you are in the studio. You're there to record your work—even your questions should be confined to that task. "Is there some way we can correct that flubbed note in the second bar?" is a legitimate question. "How are you going to correct that flub in the second bar?" is probably overstepping the bounds. You do not have to know how or why the engineer is doing what he or she does, and the engineer shouldn't have to waste time going through it with you. When musicians concern themselves with matters that shouldn't concern them, they get in their own way. Does knowing that the engineer is going to use a transformer, convert line level to mic level through impedance matching, and go in directly help you play any better? That's the question.

Here's some advice from a man who has produced more than 150 albums and knows what he's talking about:

> The key thing is not to try to master a few technical terms but to talk to the engineer in normal language. "Make it feel like we're in a big theater" or "There's too much echo" or "The bass feels wimpy, not like it does on stage" or "The snare sounds too much like a high pitched tom tom" or "That sounds great" are all perfectly fine ways to talk to your engineer. Don't try to impress everyone with what you know.

Notice that in this advice there's no reference to binaural image synthesis or proper spatial renderings of the secondary reflected sounds. By becoming heavily involved in such stuff, you may be only setting yourself up to be dragged down into the mud by the weight or your own armor, like the French at Agincourt.

When it comes to terminology, the only legitimate question for the musician is, does knowing this particular information make me a better recording artist? If it doesn't add to your ability to perform your task in the studio, then, for now at least, it's only a distraction.

Charlie Musselwhite, who has a long, impressive recording career (more than 17 albums), admits to having no knowledge of many of "the great electronic mysteries of the studio." Here's Charlie from a 1988 *Bay Blues* cover story talking about outboard equipment:

> Some of those thangs sound pretty good if they're used right. I don't use any of that stuff, but I've heard it used and thought it was kinda nice. There are some thangs, I don't even know what they are. Like a flanger. I have not a clue in my mind what a flanger is, or what it does. Or a chorus. If my life depended on it, I could not tell you what that does, or what it sounds like, or whether I would recognize one if I heard it.

Yet the lack of such information has not kept Charlie Musselwhite from being, quite possibly, the best blues harp player on the face of this planet. Nor has it prevented him from being a highly respected recording artist.

Whatever your knowledge, however, there are things that you *should* concern yourself with and things you *should not* concern yourself with. If you want to spend some time and read some technical books, it won't hurt you. But it's not necessary to the task of recording. That's the point. If you're not training to be an engineer, it's not important that you speak the engineer's lingo. What *is* important is that you have a basic understanding of what's going on. It's important that you feel comfortable with your ability to convey your needs. And it's important that you follow what the studio professionals are trying to say to you. The words in this lexicon have been selected to help you do that.

TERMS YOU SHOULD PROBABLY KNOW

absolute gain—the greatest possible gain (volume, loudness) with the least distortion and noise. Ideally, absolute gain is the *level* at which most parts are recorded.

A/D—analog-to-digital conversion.

analog—a recording method in which the sound is collected on magnetic tape. The vibrations arrange bits of metallic particles suspended on the surface of an emulsion. In playback that arrangement of the particles re-establishes the sound.

archival recordings—sometimes a recording of the entire session, more typically a copy of the master, stored at the studio for the duration of the artist's association with that studio.

attack—the speed at which a sound is detected, typically by outboard equipment.

bouncing tracks—to mix down several tracks during the tracking phase of the project in order to free up those tracks for additional recorded parts.

cans—headphones.

channel—signals coming *into* the console, or lines in (see *pick-up devices*).

clarity—retaining the sense of separation in the mix.

click track—a mechanically produced rhythm guide most commonly used by the drummer while soloing so that his timing remains good.

compression—sets a limit to the loudness. It rolls off all signals beyond whatever ceiling the engineer sets.

compressor, limiter—a device that keeps the signal from getting too loud or too soft. In the mix, used as an orchestration tool. In mastering, usually used to bring up volume on tracks that have been altered by conversion.

condenser microphones—mics that have a greater sensitivity at a distance. They either run on a battery or you need some equipment to supply phantom power. At home, for the sake of simplicity, you pretty much want to stick with dynamic mics because they have their own amplifying circuit built in and operate without any additional equipment.

cross-fade—as one channel comes up, others drop.

crossover—in speakers, sends the different frequencies to the correct speaker element, for example, high frequencies to the tweeter, lows to the woofer.

crosstalk—sound leakage from one track to another.

cue—the selected mix (of tracks or channels) to studio monitors or the artist's headphones.

D/A—digital-to-analog conversion. Sometimes digital tape is converted to an analog master.

dB—signal strength (someone said a jet plane taking off is 108 dB).

delay—the difference between the time a signal is sent and the time it is received, causing spatial effects such as echo.

depth—the fullness of the sound; fat as opposed to thin.

digital—the alternative to analog. In digital the signal is converted into a numeric code. In playback the numeric code is read and translated back into the appropriate sound.

direct box—or direct to the board, or straight into the board. An alternative to micing or sometimes a supplement to micing.

direct to digital—a method of recording either on digital audiotape or into a computer hard drive.

dispersion—the directionality of sound. Treble, for example, is very direct, with low or narrow dispersion. Bass, essentially nondirectional, has wide dispersion.

distortion—the result of a signal going beyond the dynamic range limits of the mic or any signal processor or the tape.

double tracking—playing the same piece over, either on a separate track to be mixed later or with a live mix, to create a deeper or an otherwise unobtainable, complex sound.

dry tracks—clean, without reverb or any other signal processing.

dubbing—making a copy of the tape (duplication). Sometimes the term is used casually, and incorrectly, to mean overdubbing.

ducking—the compressor calms the volume of previously recorded tracks while the track you're working with is being recorded. For example, when you want the vocals to dominate, the other tracks duck underneath the vocals.

dynamic range—the range between the lowest and the highest signal levels any device can accommodate without distortion.

EQ—used to accentuate or boost the frequency you want while eliminating frequencies you do not want. EQ eliminates the possibility of picking up stray signals, ambient sound, and crosstalk while enhancing those signals that are most crucial to the instrument's sound. For example, if you're playing a bass guitar, EQ will be used to cut out high end signals because, if there are highs coming through on that channel, they're not coming from the bass. At the same time, the EQ will be set to capture the best lows.

expander—or noise gate, re-establishes in playback what compression did while tracking.

faders—those sliding things on the control console. They control the gain (levels) on each channel.

flanging—a signal processing device that creates an elliptical kind of gain pattern, like the "whoomph whoomph" sound of those Leslie-style rotating horns in some large stage amps.

flown in—with digital recording it's easy for anyone anywhere to overdub a part and ship it, mail it, or even send it over the phone lines to the studio, where that part is added to the other tracks or flown into the mix.

fuzz—a signal processing device that intentionally pushes the signal beyond the dynamic range and distorts it.

gain—volume, loudness.

high end—high frequency, sometimes also meaning expensive. In the case of recording equipment, usually well worth the price.

keying—dedicating a particular channel to an instrument so that it's the only sound that's heard while that mic is activated. All the other channels are shut off to make the "key" instrument, or key channel, stand out.

leakage—unwanted sounds from one track recorded on another.

levels—usually the amount of gain on each track. Coupled with EQ, gain is established on high-end, mid-range, and low-end signals on each channel.

limiters—control the maximum level a signal can reach.

live mix—combining a number of channels to a fewer number of tracks during tracking, for example, while recording the rhythm section ensemble.

low-frequency transducer—a woofer or subwoofer that reproduces bass sound.

master flat—"exactly as provided." Probably no tape should ever be mastered flat. What this really means is that the mastering lab accepts no responsibility for the results.

mute—to silence a track so that you can listen to another track, or combination of tracks, without changing the levels of those tracks. In the mix it's used to keep noise from a track out of the mix until the desired signal comes up. For example, if at some point in the tune, a section of horns surfaces, you mute the track the horns are on until it's time for them to come up, and you mute that track again after the horns fade.

noise—unwanted sound. Amplifiers, the recording machine, playback devices, speakers, and even cable generate noise simply through the process of functioning. Ambient sound can also be noise if it's in there and it's not wanted.

noise reduction—one of several patented systems by which noise created by the machines involved in the recording process itself is prevented from being recorded. Whatever the technical details (someone said something about a controlled algorithm), noise reduction alters the signal while tracking and then restores the signal in playback. If you track using noise reduction, and do not use it in playback, something vital will be missing in playback. Noise reduction is one of those topics about which far too many people claim to be experts.

overdubbing—recording an additional track to tracks already recorded, such as when a vocalist listens to the rhythm tracks and lays down a vocal track

panning—from the word *panorama*. A pan pot sends the signal *anywhere* throughout a 180-degree sound field, typically, left, right, or center.

phasers—double the sound but place the second version out of synch.

pickup devices—microphones, direct boxes, pickups (see *channel*).

premix—when the signal from more than one input/channel is recorded on one track.

punch—the perceived impact a sound has, usually relating to drums.

punch in—a method for taping over a mistake by playing along with the recorded track until the mistake comes up, at which point the engineer *punches in* and records while the performer plays the correction. When the correction is complete, the engineer *punches out*. Done successfully, the results are referred to as *seamless*.

reference recordings—or scratch track, a track recorded, probably to be scrapped later, so that other instruments know where they're at in the tune. For example, a reference or scratch vocal may be recorded at about the same time as the basic tracks so that other musicians who are used to hearing the vocals on that tune don't get lost.

release—the time within which a signal is no longer being processed. Typically used with compression, limiter/expander.

reverb—sometimes referred to as *talent*. Every vocalist knows the benefits of reverb. It creates the apparent space the sound is in, whether a broom closet or the Grand Canyon. Poor vocalists usually sound better in the latter.

riding gain—making gain adjustments while the track is being recorded. Riding gain is an important part of orchestration in the mix.

rough mix—a temporary mix of tracks to cassette, done so that the musicians have something to take home, study, pick apart, argue over, or beam about.

running log/session log—a log or chart (or sometimes only notes) of a recording session. It may have each take listed, who played, EQ settings, the name of each tune, the date of the session—any and all details the engineer feels might be of use in future, related sessions.

separation—maximum separation is best achieved by recording tracks solo. In order to eliminate crosstalk, each instrument is recorded separately with baffles or isolated in separate rooms so that no ambient (stray) sound is picked up on that track.

signal processing devices—outboard electronic devices that alter the signal, phasers, flangers, compressors, limiters, reverb.

slate—a start notation for each take. When the engineer says, "Take one," it's so the mastering engineer, for example, knows which take is about to be played.

solo—a function on the board that lets you listen to one channel without affecting the other channels in order to check or make adjustments to that channel, or listen to a single track through the studio monitors or headphones without affecting other tracks.

soloing—when a single instrument or voice is recorded alone in the studio. The point is isolation of the signal and separation of tracks. Best achieved by recording in an acoustically "dead" studio.

tape machine—the big unit, not the ones built for duplication, not the deck you have in your car.

tip-ring sleeve—a literal description of a 1/4-inch stereo jack. Guitar jacks (which are mono) are tip-sleeve.

track—separate physical tracks recorded on the tape.

tracking—recording.

track sheet or tape log—a record of what's on each track (*track assignment*), what mics are used, the EQ, the outboard settings.

transmission devices—typically cables, but also wireless. The console itself—anything that carries the signal to another device.

trim control—used to boost gain.

tweak—manipulate the sound through the board or through signal processing equipment. To set the EQ so that upper mid-range comes across stronger, or to fatten it up with digital delay, is *tweaking* the mid-range.

washed out—when the definition of a sound is lost in too much reverb.

XLR connector—three-pin connector common to low-impedance microphones.

OTHER THINGS YOU SHOULD KNOW

Amplifiers, the recording machine, playback devices, speakers, even cables are rated according to their limitations. They each have their own range of sounds they respond to (frequency response) and can handle without distortion (dynamic range). They all add noise of their own simply through the process of functioning.

Once something is on tape, it can be converted to digital, reproduced, edited, amplified, or processed. This means, generally, that you can and probably should record as clean as possible and make such adjustments later.

In most studios the best monitors available are used to ensure that the engineer is attaining the finest sound possible. But cheap speakers are also used to see how your stuff might sound coming over an AM radio at the beach. No matter how pure the sound on high-end speakers, it can come across extremely harsh on smaller, cheaper speakers. The best advice, from the best people in the business, is to take every opportunity to listen to your work on different speakers. Listen to it on different studio monitors, listen to it on your car tape deck, listen to it at home, listen to it in different environments.

Digital is loaded in real time, whether it's going into a computer for editing or going to analog tape or being duplicated.

All tape is calibrated to be played back on decks with corresponding settings. What this means to you is that you need the right tape for whatever machine you're using. And wherever the tape goes, the calibrations need to go too.

A LITTLE LEXICON STORY

I wandered in on a session late one night in which some kids were making some pretty neat music. It was a little four-piece rock unit, and they were tracking vocals over the top. When I heard what was coming out over the monitors, I thought, "This ought to be interesting; these kids are really tight." It was interesting all right, but not in the way I'd anticipated.

In ensemble work, when it's *really* working, unusual harmonics sometimes occur during tracking. Added voicings are revealed on tape that artists may be unaware of until they hear them for the first time through the headphones. I'm sure musicologists have a name for this gestalt of sound—perhaps overtone—maybe it's just harmony. If you're not accustomed to hearing your music in a studio setting, unmixed and played back at high gain, these harmonics can sound quite strange. They can, in fact, sound like something is terribly wrong. Actually, however, they are usually an indication of just how well things are going. "All discord is harmony not understood" (Alexander Pope).

Harmonizing vocalists sometimes give such a phenomenon a personal name—for example, "Lucy"—so they can refer to it while critiquing takes. When Lucy shows up, it means the vocals are working perfectly. During this session the rhythmic meshing of the tracks was generating Lucy. That's how good these kids were. That's how well the recording was coming along. Both the musicians and the engineer had done a nice job.

The lead singer was having a serious problem with Lucy, however. He kept stopping midtake to complain, "Man, what is that *noise*?" The engineer assured him that everything was going great and encouraged him to continue. But the "noise" was driving the singer wild. He'd start in again, only to stop after a couple of bars and demand, "You honestly can't hear that?"

The engineer rolled back the tape and listened, but all he could detect was synchronized ensemble music captured nicely. To him such sounds were an indication of successful recording; he couldn't find evidence of noise anywhere. Clearly, if he'd had any idea what "noise" the vocalist was referring to, he would have simply eliminated it from the singer's headphones. Rather than go through a struggle of this sort, any engineer will gladly turn a couple of knobs.

In the studio the artist was beginning to question the engineer's abilities. He was worried that the guy might be screwing up their project. He was frustrated because he didn't know where the "noise" was coming from. He only knew it wasn't the sound of the bass and it wasn't the sound of the guitar. He knew it wasn't a drum sound. He also knew he wasn't making it. In his mind it had to be a screw-up of some sort. He began shaking his head and muttering (through an open mic), "I don't know how anyone could not hear that fucking noise."

The engineer rolled back tape and offered playback as proof of the fact that there was no noise. But for the singer each playback only confirmed the undeniable presence of the noise. This went on until the engineer began to tire of it. He resented the questioning of his expertise and was becoming irritated by the repeated disruption. Resentment started to come across in his voice.

What was going on was obvious to me. It was literally a matter of semantics. As an uninvited guest, however, I was not about to dive into the fray. Trying to explain things to a kid so green that he didn't know good recording when he heard it seemed futile. I was even less inclined to attempt to explain what I thought the problem might be to a professional sound engineer. Consequently, this humiliating scene went on for a while.

Finally the singer whipped off his headphones, jumped down from his barstool, came charging out of the studio into the control booth, leaned with both palms on the console, looked the engineer in the face, and started making demands. He was pretty explicit about it. He didn't want "that fucking noise" on his "fucking record." As a paying customer, he demanded that it be tracked down and eliminated. He stood up, stepped back, and repeated his demand for the sake of those in distant lands with hearing problems.

The engineer responded wearily, "I'd be glad to do something about it, but quite frankly, I don't know what you're talking about." He stopped short of adding "and I don't think you do either." The room was getting pretty chilly, even for a recording studio.

Typically, problems in the studio start out small and escalate throughout the project. So this one had probably been festering for a while. What was peculiar in all of this was that the recording was going really well. That noise, in fact, was an indication of just how well the thing was going. But nothing the engineer could have said or done would have convinced the vocalist of that.

For a minute it looked like a brawl was about to break out. The drummer came flying up out of his chair, pointed his finger in a somewhat threatening manner at the engineer's face, and said, "Hey, man . . . !" While he quivered there, trying to properly frame the rest of his thought, I decided it was time for me to quietly slip away. No doubt they'd be rolling back the tape, going over it and over it again. Even with everyone in a good mood, that sort of thing soon grows tiresome. I didn't want to be there while the process dragged on.

More important, though, I didn't want to be there to witness the scene when it finally dawned on the engineer which "noise" the kid was worried about and he was forced to explain, "Why, you little idiot, that's a *good* noise."

This is a classic example of the fact that the engineer's perspective and the musician's perspective are often two very different things. This was more than merely a debate over the definition of *noise,* however. Also at issue were what constitutes good recording, who's in control in the recording studio, and how problems should be resolved. In short, the vocalist was in there recording music, while the engineer was there to record sound. *That's* generally the problem. The engineer is listening for sound quality; the artist, for music.

In the studio we have an artist—exposed, open, vulnerable—offering up the labors of his or her heart. In the booth is a person focusing on things like stereo image stability and phase integrity while worrying about arbitrary signal collapse. In this case, as in most cases, the engineer had the advantage of years of experience and a finely tuned ear, not to mention a quarter million dollars' worth of electronics to continually monitor the state of the signal.

In the eternal confrontation between art and technology, technology usually wins. "I just feel that it needs more . . . well, you know, more, uh . . . presence" can't stand up against "a fixed point DSP processing platform designed to avoid different implementations offering differing rounding errors in preset integrals." That's why such debates are not only a waste of time but also usually a losing battle for the artist.

Naturally, the artist embroiled in such a mess is frustrated (in this case infuriated). It can be embarrassing not to be able to communicate your needs. For the engineer, though, it is just another unnecessary waste of studio time brought on by the musician's limited understanding of the process.

Even in the best working situation, separate views about what's going on can turn antagonistic, counterproductive, even mutually exclusive. In the studio, many times the artist is purposefully kept unaware of any possible developing conflict. Studio personnel usually bow quietly to the artist's demands—after all, that's who is paying the bills.

The real problem with conflict in the studio is that if things are going too badly, the staff may want to simply get the session over with. And that is not the attitude you want them to have while working on your project.

When it's working, the sometimes volatile collision of these two extreme viewpoints ensures that the work gets done well. Both points of view—the (emotional) aesthetic and the (coldly) technical—are equally valuable in the production of good recorded music. The forced melding of somewhat opposing iron wills—"mad as the sea and wind when both contend which is the mightier"—can produce magnificent results.

Such magnificence *is* possible even for artists going into the studio for the first time. It's more likely to occur, however, when the artist surrenders to the way the recording studio is run and respects the knowledge of studio professionals. It's amazing what can be done to alter and correct flaws when the person operating the equipment feels good about the artist.

5

················
LOGISTICS
························

Coming across in the studio in a professional manner means arriving ready to play. Arriving ready to play is largely a matter of logistics and preproduction. Even before setting foot in the studio, you can help yourself considerably if you sit down with a pencil and paper. "The readiness is all."

The first thing to do is work out your budget and project schedule. (Samples of each are found at the end of this book.) It's important to write down anything that you might want to ask the studio staff before things get underway. It's also important to write such things down throughout the duration of the project. Equally important, of course, is to follow up. Ask those questions.

PREPRODUCTION

Preproduction is everything you should do before you arrive at the studio, and a few things afterward. In the strictest sense, preproduction refers to song preparation. But everything you do before you go in—to make going into the studio possible, workable, bearable, enjoyable, and successful—is preproduction. This includes working out your budget and drawing up a project schedule, as well as song preparation. In general, whatever time you take up front, in preproduction, affects the amount of time you'll spend tracking and in the mix.

Studio professionals confess their continual amazement at how unprepared many musicians are for going into the studio. "They come in, and the band hasn't bothered to plan, hasn't bothered to prepare, check their equipment, get the amps fixed, or change strings. They don't arrive on time, don't remember to bring their guitar cord, don't remember to bring drumsticks, yet they expect to record." It's an all-too-common scenario.

BUDGET

For their budget, some musicians only determine how many sessions they think they might need to record. Others simply calculate how many hours they can get in the studio for the money they have. There are other matters to consider. Your budget needs to account for preproduction, all studio sessions (tracking), post-production (mixing, editing, sequencing, mastering, and tape transfers), and post-postproduction (manufacture, packaging, and distribution).

When you define every aspect of this process specifically, you are less likely to be surprised by unexpected expenses. It helps sometimes to think things through backward, at each step considering smaller details. When you think of tapes, think of labels. When you think of labels, think of printing them. When you think of printing them, think of what it might cost to have them prepared nicely on a computer.

Before you go in, you need to consider the cost of things like instrument setup, extra parts—strings, cords, drum heads, tubes—lead sheets. If you're planning to use studio instruments, don't forget to add in their cost.

After the project is complete in the studio, the work (postproduction) has really just begun. The final mix you'll come away with will be no good to you whatsoever unless you've set aside the bucks to master it, press it, and launch some sort of distribution (if that's what you plan to do). Consider, too, the cost of art, text, graphics for J cards or CDV cards, and band photos. Factor in printing, labeling, packing, and shipping.

While budgeting, don't forget about the cost of tape. The two-track master of the final mix may be offered as part of the studio's service (and sometimes a safety as well). You will be expected to pay for everything else, including the tape you track on. Some studios will give you the rough mix from each session on cassette and simply add the cassette cost to your bill; others will ask you to supply the blank tape. If everyone in the band wants copies, expect to see that reflected on your bill. Unless you have specific information otherwise, assume you're going to pay for any and all tape you use in the studio and for all time spent duplicating tape. Just because you're not in the studio doesn't mean work isn't being done on your project and you're not being billed for it.

For strictly political reasons, you may want to buy the tape from the studio, even if it costs a little more. Anytime you supply tape—even if it's just cassettes—ask the engineer what kind of tape to get. If it's a brand name, buy it. If you bring in something the engineer is not set up to use, any time spent on setup and adjustments of the recording machine (things that are normally done before you arrive) will be done on your time, while you wait.

If you go analog on 2-inch tape and you buy it yourself, there are two standard lengths. You get approximately 30 minutes of recording time on a short roll of 2-inch tape. At this writing, it goes for around $150. There is no great savings in buying the long reel, although it will afford you more uninterrupted tracking time (depending upon taping speed, 10 to 15 minutes more). Be aware that the longer reel is more subject to wow and flutter and other such tape- or tape-machine-related distortions. That's the toss-up. Longer, uninterrupted recording time is coupled with the greater possibility of a glitch.

In the end, the final mix is yours. But if you decide to convert it to some other format, you can expect to pay for that conversion. Everyone suggests that you store a safety on DAT, and most mastering houses prefer a DAT master. If it's going to or coming from digital, remember that digital is loaded into a computer for editing, conversion, and transfer in real time. You will be charged by the hour.

Somewhere in your budget you need to include mechanical licensing fees for covers (other people's material) and copyright fees for securing your own tunes. Studios traditionally have a hands-off view of things like registering copyright, paying musicians' union fees, securing mechanical rights, and duplicating or converting your master after you have it in hand. Be prepared to handle these things yourself. Think about them and get them underway before you go into the studio.

SCHEDULING

In order to complete your project in some reasonable, timely manner, lay out a project schedule. Scheduling can be tricky because it depends on so many variables. Typically, the schedule will need adjustment during the project. After all, in multitracking we're talking about making reference tracks and basic tracks, editing and bouncing basic tracks, overdubbing key pieces, adding sweetener, editing, and mixing down. Unless you work out a project schedule and attempt to stick to it, you may find the project delayed, or worse, the project may never reach completion.

Scheduling is based on how much stuff you plan to record, how complex the music is, the format you plan to use (analog or digital), and how you plan to record it (how much will be ensemble and how much solo), all of which affect the time it will take to track and mix. If you haven't decided on any of this, talk to the engineer beforehand. Ask for advice about how best to go about recording your work.

To say that you're going to book five sessions and record three tunes is not enough. You need to determine what specifically is going to take place during each of those sessions. The project schedule delineates which instruments will be recording which parts of which tunes on which day. By creating such a schedule, you will determine who's going to be in on that session and, just as important, who is not.

Determining how much time you'll need in the studio is something like picking a race horse. No matter how bizarre or well informed your approach, you'll probably end up tantalizingly close but still wrong. The rule of thumb for estimating time spent tracking (according to one engineer) is "Take the worst possible case scenario, assume everything that can go wrong will, add 20 percent, and multiply by pi, because you'll probably be going around in circles for a while." As whimsical as that may appear on the surface, it's probably as good a method as any until you have accumulated some experience.

Don't think that one hour of studio time translates into one hour of tape. Nothing could be further from the truth. Typically, the first hour (or even two) of studio time in each session translates into no tape at all. That time is gobbled up in arrival, setup, testing, adjusting levels, warmup, and run-throughs (with further adjustments) before any tracking takes place. Drums and vocalists will both require special attention during setup and initial tracking. Other instruments are usually somewhat more predictable, and the staff can set up for them in advance of your arrival.

During tracking you can expect continual adjustments, minor squabbles, lengthy discussions over matters that will ultimately prove insignificant, playback, false starts, breaks, and necessary technical delays.

Some people consider any session a success if they get one good take of whatever they are in there to do that day. If they get two good takes to choose between, it's an overwhelming success. Others advise that if you get three good takes right out of the box, wrap it up—you've done a day's work. I'd suggest that if you get two or three good takes right out of the box, keep going. When the magic's working, work the magic.

The myth, of course, is that you're going to go in and crank out enough tunes for an album in one session. What is too eagerly overlooked in that daydream is the fact that most professionals, people with years of studio experience, take months, a year, two years, four years, forever to come out of the studio with enough tape for an album. The idea that you can go in there and slap together an album in one or two quick sessions is only going to cause you trouble. It's not going to happen. When it doesn't, where does that leave you? You're disappointed, you're frustrated, you may be a little embarrassed. You may begin to question your own abilities and the abilities of your fellow musicians. That's a terrible way to feel. It's not conducive to playing, let alone recording. That's why it's always better to limit what you intend to do in the studio.

The reality is, if you go into the studio the first time hoping to come away with two or three good songs ready for the mix, you have a pretty good chance of making that happen.

Your first time in is a learning experience. So consider scheduling five four-hour-long sessions and see where that gets you. For ensemble recording, five sessions include one or two sessions for laying down the basic tracks (for up to three tunes), one or two sessions for tracking harmonies, vocals, and instrumental solos, and a fifth session for sweetener. Mixing will require additional studio time.

While you're considering these things, you should know that the last session on the calendar for any given date is usually the only one available for overtime.

What you really want to do your first time in is to gain some understanding of how much time it takes to record your work. This will help you schedule future projects. Unless you're used to it, six hours is an extremely long time to spend in the studio. So think in terms of four-hour-long sessions. At times, four hours can be grueling. On the other hand, you may discover that time just flies by and four hours doesn't seem like enough time for you. I know this much: anyone who tells you, "Man, we were in the studio till dawn," either wasted a lot of time in there or arrived at 3:00 A.M.

When scheduling vocalists, consider three hours at the most. If the vocalist doesn't finish in three, send him or her away. It's a rare vocalist who can rev the vocal cords for three hours without burning up the clutch. If there is some extra time, you might want to listen to playback and assess where you stand. If the vocalist simply comes in and nails it and you have a couple of hours left, there may be enough time to set up quickly to correct some flaws.

If things go absolutely 100 percent perfectly, tracking for three tunes could reasonably be complete in two or three sessions. But it's unlikely. It depends, of course, on how complex the music is, how much overdubbing you plan to do, and how quickly you adjust to the pressures of recording.

Pencil in the first couple of sessions to set up and record the rhythm section. Then just go in and lay down as many rhythm tracks as possible in the first session. In five days you may have satisfactorily recorded your entire repertoire. If so, good. Start laying down the bed tracks for the next project.

You do not want to put too much time pressure on yourself the first time in the studio. The way to avoid this is not by booking an infinite number of endless sessions but by limiting the amount of stuff you plan to do in the studio. One tune can be considered a successful project if you come away with good results.

On the other hand, you do not want to run out of time in the middle of the project. If you run out of time, the studio may not be able to get you in again for a week or two, a month or two, a decade or two, and that can put a little kink in the momentum. So it's better to overbook. Five sessions is not exactly overbooking, but it *is* enough time to get some real work done if you stay on schedule. Again, once you've drawn up a project schedule, attempt to stick to it as much as possible.

Remember, if at any time during the project you think about canceling a session, it's a very costly thing to do. If you've already paid for the time, you can kiss that money goodbye. If you've scheduled only five sessions, scrapping one of them isn't going to help alleviate the pressures of time. Canceling not only screws up the project but is also unprofessional. This is yet another good reason to find a studio with a convenient location. If it's easy to get to, you're less likely to cancel.

Rest assured that the studio is not going to let you down. If you're scheduled to be there, the studio staff will be there. The sole exception is thunderstorms. Many studios shut down during thunderstorms rather than risk a lightning strike. Whatever protection surge protectors and voltage regulators are designed to offer, valuable projects and a couple of hundred thousand dollars' worth of high end recording equipment are considered by most to be worth the cost of a few lost hours. In such weather you might call ahead. Otherwise, if you are slated to be there, be there. A no-show offends studio professionals.

With your project schedule in hand, make a list of all the things you need to do before going into the studio for each session. List the musicians for each session on your schedule, and if you are in a band, make it clear that only those musicians who are working during the session are to attend. Generally speaking, once you're slated to go into the studio, it's too late for rehearsal. However, if you've got any time before you are scheduled to go in, rehearse, rehearse, rehearse. Get your repertoire together.

EQUIPMENT PREPARATION

As soon as you get your project schedule in place, start preparing your equipment for the studio. You want to go in with your equipment in working order. This means tuneable, playable, *professionally* set up, all the parts there and functioning. You should have all your back-up parts too (strings, fuses, cords, fittings, drum heads, and such). Make a list of all equipment according to which musician may need it. If there is anything missing or in need of fixing—get it taken care of. You might want to list the instruments required at each session on your project schedule and check them out before going in.

When you take your stuff to a repair shop, be sure to tell them you're going into the studio. Then they'll set up the instruments with that consideration in mind, looking for grounding problems, cable shielding problems, vacuum leaks—things that might not matter on stage and they might not have checked for otherwise. Once an instrument is isolated, all kinds of problems that you were not aware of can crop up.

The professionally set-up instrument should look, play, and sound better than it did before it went in. When you get your equipment back, tape each piece, solo, in a quiet room and listen carefully to that tape. If problems show up on the tape, track them down and correct them or take the instrument back in. If you take it back to the repair shop, take the tape with you. It will help to demonstrate what you're concerned about. Be diplomatic, though. A nicely set-up instrument sometimes reveals otherwise unexposed weaknesses in the artist's musicianship.

SONG PREPARATION

When recording studio professionals make comments about musicians coming in unprepared, what they are usually saying is that the musicians don't have their repertoire together. They haven't selected which pieces they're going to do and are not prepared to present them. If you follow the advice in this chapter on preparation, you will be prepared, and whether or not studio staff is impressed with your music, they'll certainly be impressed with your approach to the work. If there is one thing all studio professionals have in common, it is a work ethic.

Your first time in the studio, aim at getting three songs down. Three tunes is an entirely reasonable goal to set for yourself first time in. This is something that can be accomplished. It's not an overwhelming project, but it's large enough to give you a very good idea of how things go in the studio when dealing with your work. And it's a respectable accomplishment. If you go in and nail three tunes, you can feel proud of yourself.

Many professional recording artists record in a similar manner, especially while on tour. They prepare their tunes on stage, set up the musicians and studio in a town slated for later in the tour, and shoot a tape ahead to everyone who will be involved. When they get into town, they go into the studio and cut two or three tunes. When they feel that a few more tunes are ready to go, they book another studio somewhere down the road, round up musicians by phone, shoot them tapes of the stuff they plan to record. When they get to that town, they go in and record those select tunes.

For Charlie Musselwhite, who used to tour "only about 300 days a year" but these days finds himself "doin' a year a week," recording while touring is the only way for him to produce an album. Charlie's recent album, on Pointblank Records, was recorded in just that manner. He used different musicians and different producers in Chicago, L.A., and New Orleans. "You do a few tunes here and a few there, and it adds up enough to be one album. . . . The main thing is, you don't want to waste any time in there. If you're really prepared, completely rehearsed, and everything and everybody in the band knows the tunes, you can just go in and burn tape."

When you go in, which tunes you're planning to do should be established. Select your three best songs. Any more than that, for your first project, can only lead to trouble. For now, your best songs are the ones that you always feel comfortable playing, songs that you enjoy playing and that seem to work nicely every time. Write these tunes down. List them in order. Those are the songs you're going to rehearse if you have any time before going into the studio. Call them your project tunes. If these songs do not have names, give them names.

Then find three tunes that you know are good, tunes that you like but might need a little work. Call them back-up tunes. If these songs are nameless, give them names. Write them down. These are the songs you'll work on at home while in the studio recording your project tunes.

Strangely enough, hours of exhaustive studio work may leave you with an unquenchable urge to play after you leave the studio. After a seemingly endless session, you may find yourself pacing the floor, chomping at the bit, eager to continue. This is the time to turn your attention to your back-up tunes and develop their routine. If things work out perfectly and you nail the first three tunes in a timely manner, you'll have these back-up tunes in place, ready to go.

All other songs—songs that give you any kind of difficulty whatsoever, songs that you're still working on, songs that you're not sure about—should be forgotten. As long as you are working on a studio project, you should not waste time on any other songs. Concentrate solely on the project tunes while in the studio and on the back-up tunes, if you have time, outside.

Always rehearse your project tunes in the same way you plan to record them: in the same order, same arrangement, same tempo. Use the same instruments and the same setup. For example, have your drummer practice with the bass-drum skin removed and with damper rings. If you are going to multitrack, get the rhythm section in there rehearsing the rhythm part alone. Tape that session and have the lead instruments rehearse to that tape.

The reason the rhythm track is laid down first—and the reason it is called a bed track—is that all other tracks are built on top of it. So it's important that the rhythm arrangement be solidly routine. Tempo is especially important. The bed track establishes the tempo that all takes from then on will match. This is a crucial point. In editing, when you attempt to replace a poor passage with a better take of that same passage, the tempos must conform. That's one of the reasons drums alone can take an entire session.

Have the vocalist rehearse to a rough mix of the rhythm tracks—if possible, with the tape playing through headphones. In rehearsal, play through mistakes and grind away at it until you have several good takes. Then move on to the next tune and approach it in the same way. Rehearsing at home in the same way you plan to track in the studio will help you to prepare yourself.

The recording studio is for recording. It's not a place to practice, finalize arrangements, write lyrics, or make decisions about which version of a song you will do. All of these things should be done at home, before you go in.

ROUTINING

Your engineer may need to know where a song is going in order to see that it gets there. So each song must be routine, locked in, set. This means you have decided:

- Which key each song is in
- The tempo it will be played at
- Which particular version you will be doing (if you have more than one arrangement)

In addition you have:

- Finalized the lyrics
- Anticipated effects and sweetener

Resolve all of these things at home. "These are the tunes we're going to do, and this is the way we're going to do them." Once your project songs are routine, do not change anything. Now is *not* the time to make changes. Do not change tempo, arrangements, your song list, the order of play. Add no new equipment. Do not work on new lyrics. Stick with what you've been working on.

It's always tempting to go in and just wing it in the studio. Don't. Go into the studio to do what you've prepared yourself to do.

Lowell Fulson is a man with 50 years of recording experience. He is an inspiring guitar player and a monumental talent. Performers as diverse as Pee-Wee Crayton and Robben Ford have acknowledged him as a major influence in their work. In a *Bay Blues* interview in 1989, I asked Fulson, "You open up in a break, do you ever play the same solo twice?"

He responded, "It's a little different sometimes. Sometimes, you make it a little stronger, or you make it better by adding a little something to it, so it's a bit different. 'Course very few people pick a perfect solo every time."

The obvious follow-up question was "That sounds like you have something very specific in mind to fill that break. You have a precise, note for note thang that you try to play each time, is that it?"

Answer: "Yeah. Yeah."

Here we were talking about live performance. But certainly if Lowell Fulson takes that kind of routine approach to stage work, you can safely predict that his solos are also routined before he goes into the recording studio.

Listen to what Dick Shurman says about Edgar Winter and see if you think Winter's work might be routined. "I had one chance to work with Edgar Winter, on a Johnny Winter project, and he really impressed me as a consummate studio musician. One of the things that impressed me so much about him was you could tell him to do something just the way he did it the last time, just change one thing about it. And he could play that, just exactly like he did it before, with only that one thing changed. Not everybody can do that . . . and with most people, you shouldn't even try."

As an artist, you might be concerned that routining might deaden the feeling behind a solo or deprive you of taking it as far as you possibly can. That's a legitimate concern. I'd like to suggest that routining your work does just the opposite. Contrary to what one might suppose, routining your work does not stifle your creativity—it enhances it.

The proof can be found by listening to artists like Lowell Fulson and Edgar Winter on record. Fulson's guitar work always comes across fresh, innovative, strong, sensitive. Winter's work always comes across sounding spontaneous and inspired. It's the routine approach that allows Fulson to move around in there comfortably, making it "better by adding a little something to it." Routining makes it possible for Winter to play everything exactly as before, changing only one thing, without losing it altogether.

Anyone who has ever worked days on end to learn a piece from a record knows that it's the nuance that makes the difference. It's not just the slurs, the bends, the vibrato, the sustains—it's the quality of these things. What separates Miles Davis from any other horn player playing the exact same piece, note for note, is the sensitivity Miles brings to it. The tighter your routine, the more precise your focus becomes and, consequently, the more sensitive you can be to nuance. If your stuff isn't routine, you never know what you're gonna get. If it is routine, you are only one step away from brilliance.

With your routine established, prepare lead sheets for each tune. These sheets should show the name of the tune, key signature, tempo, chord progressions, and melody line. It will help the engineer if you also supply a lyric sheet with all of the lyrics typed on a separate page, double or triple spaced to leave room for scribbling notes. If the tune is instrumental, prepare a form guide, something the engineer can make notes on: intro, rhythm section, piano solo, horn section, strings surface, strings diminish, horns again, outro. These sheets not only will help the engineer but will also help keep the project on schedule. If you have someone do this work for you, pay a flat fee.

A WORD OF CAUTION

Producers, managers, and people who make connections for you should all be paid in full at the time they render their services. Artists who are not yet signed often make the mistake of offering a percentage of future earnings in return for such immediate favors. That's a tempting way to go, but it can prove to be a big mistake. When you do start earning, you'll discover just how big. Some artists go into their first recording contract with weasels of every stripe clinging to them, each one bleeding them for 10 percent for some minor favor rendered while the artist was still struggling.

You'd be amazed at how watertight the simplest contract can prove to be. The most casual supportive gesture can quickly transform itself into a cold-hearted business agreement. Polonius had it right: neither a borrower nor a lender be. Never offer anyone a percentage of your future. I know a good horn player who offered such a deal to his fans. Although still a good horn player, he is now also considered a liar by some, a phony by others, and a thief by people who previously loved his work. Worse, I think somewhere in the back of his mind this debt to his former fans and friends must haunt him.

RIGHTS

One question that everybody asks is about the rights to other people's songs. The answer is simple. If you are planning to sell something with someone else's work on it, you need to obtain a *mechanical rights license* to use that material and you need to pay royalties on every unit sold.

It's equally important to protect the rights to your own songs. This is the sort of thing that many people put off and hope to forget about. But it won't go away simply because you've ignored it. If you expect to make money from your songs, you cannot reasonably, at the same time, try to avoid paying others for the use of their songs. So take Aretha Franklin's advice, show a little respect and take care of business.

If you plan to use someone else's work, contact that person's publisher directly. If you cannot find the publisher, contact the Harry Fox Agency. Harry Fox represents something like 90 percent of all music publishers in the United States, administering mechanical licenses for more than 6,000 publishers.

There is a standard established rate for the use of tunes. In September 1996 it was 6.6 cents per composition for each unit distributed (that rate was slated to expire at the end of 1997). I'm told that if you contact the publisher directly, you can negotiate a reduced rate—labels rarely pay more than 75 percent of the rate themselves. Royalties are due quarterly. However, the pay schedule is flexible and individually negotiable.

Call Harry Fox at (212) 370-5330, and they'll send you a neat, highly readable, easily understood 30-page booklet that explains everything. Harry Fox has a deal for you if you plan on distributing 500 units or less. For $34.75 per tune, you can get the rights to use any tune.

What happens if you don't do this and the fact surfaces? If you do not obtain the rights and you use other people's material, it's called piracy. That's what you don't want other people doing with your work. Ever since Puccini hit New York—and discovered his opera being performed without royalties being paid—rights of this sort have been viciously defended in court. When Led Zepp ripped off a Willie Dixon tune, "You Need Love," and turned it into the monster hit "Whole Lotta Love," ultimately all they did was to fund Dixon's Blues Heaven Foundation—an organization that puts free harmonicas into the hands of young schoolchildren. That probably was not first on the list of things Zepp thought they'd like to do with that money.

The point is, if they get you and they take you to court, they're going to make an example out of you. Willful infringement will cost you up to a $25,000 fine and possible jail time.

Harry Fox tells me that if you apply for mechanical rights after the fact, Harry Fox will accept your payment, but the publisher still has the right to nail you for infringement. So secure the mechanical rights to tunes as soon as you have decided your product is going to be made commercially available.

PROTECTING YOUR OWN WORK

According to the most recent laws, you do not have to register your work with the Copyright Office. Your work doesn't even need to bear a copyright notice. However, one of the things that such notice does is to subtly convey the message to others that you are aware of your rights. It serves as a warning.

If you find yourself in a quibble over ownership, your work must be registered before you go to court. This can be done after the fact. It's better all around, however, to file when you write the song because it attaches an officially recognized date to the creation of your work. If two people show up in court with the same lyrics or the same progression and the same melody line, the one who can demonstrate that he or she did it first is generally the person who wins.

To register your own work, write to:

Copyright Office
Library of Congress
Washington DC 20559

Or call "The Copyright Hot-line" at (202) 707-9100. This is basically a tape-recorded ordering system for those who know what forms they want. The uninformed have to call (202) 707-3000 and are given the standard run-around before being allowed the privilege of going mano a mano with a bitter, snappish, begrudgingly cooperative federal employee.

Ask for Form PA (Performing Arts: published and unpublished musical works) and Form SR (Sound Recording: published or unpublished sound recordings). For as long as I can remember, the fee has been $10 for each application. All you have to do is fill out the forms, enclose the fee, and shoot them a cassette with as much material as you can cram on it.

Officially the copyright folks call such a collection of works a *compilation*. The cassette itself is called a deposit. Your original musical composition, submitted for copyright purposes, is a phonorecord. Be sure to list the individual tunes as part of the whole and save copies for your own purposes. And don't worry, you can sell the rights, in part or in whole, to any particular piece on that compilation.

Some artists I know make a habit of filling up a cassette with their newest pieces on a regular basis and shooting it off for registration. Unless the work is being distributed, it is considered unpublished, but such unpublished works, when they do become commercially available, do not require further copyright.

The finished product from your studio sessions (album, tape, CD), whether the tunes are your original work or someone else's, is a sound recording. You will want to fill out the appropriate forms and pay the fee to copyright the sound recording.

THREE DAYS BEFORE

Three days before going in, call the studio and make sure you've got the time correct and they've got you slated. Tell the engineer what you plan to do during that session and what instruments are to be recorded. Check out all of your equipment. Gather everything you might be using and make a complete list. Be methodical about it. Write down everything you will need, including spare cords, spare fuses, extra sets of strings, drum heads, reeds, drum sticks and other back-up items. If there is anything you may need but do not have, go out and get it.

This is the time to change all strings and reeds and drum heads so that they've adjusted a bit before being used in the studio. Make sure all cables and fittings work. Check out these things in a quiet room. Listen for any buzzes, pops, clicks, squeaks, hums. These otherwise acceptable sounds will not work in the studio. This is the time to make sure all adjustment knobs work, that you know which cord gets plugged into which receptacle, that you have enough rosin, or the right picks. If you have a favorite shirt, and that sort of thing is important to you, make sure it's rumpled, ripped, and ready to go.

From this day on, make no changes to anything. Do not change the routine for any song, don't add a drum, don't decide that now's a good time to try out that new flanger, don't change jobs or living arrangements, don't get involved in any other project, don't see how you might like the drums set up on your left instead of your right, don't sing sitting down if you're used to singing standing up. Change nothing.

When you go in, *everything* should be routine.

Make your decisions about what songs you are going to do. Decide how you're going to do them, in what order, how you're going to set up, what the lyrics are, and whether the second tune ends on a booming sustain or an ice-cold vibrato. Then stick to your decisions. Mayhem does, at times, occur in the studio despite all preparation, but you have a better chance of avoiding much of it if you plan ahead.

Time will disappear once you're in the studio. Laying out a plan and sticking with it can only help your project to be completed successfully on time.

If you're working with a band, it's especially important to make sure that everybody is in agreement about what you're planning to do, how you're going to do it, where it's going to take place and when. You might want to see that everyone involved has a copy of your project schedule. Or that a copy is hung up somewhere where everyone can refer to it. If any members of the group are the sort who require whacking over the head in order to get their full attention, now's the time to start whacking.

If you know from rehearsals that somebody might have an attitude problem, then you've got a problem that needs to be resolved before going in. If it looks like you may end up wanting that person out of the studio, now's the time to figure out how you're going to go about that and who you can get as a replacement. It might be a good idea to place some calls and see who might be available to step in if it comes to that. With a band all that stuff should be ironed out before you go into the studio.

If you haven't already done so, it's now absolutely necessary to appoint a producer. If you're assuming that the studio engineer will act as producer, you'd better be sure that person is willing to accept the role. You will need someone in place with a cool head and an objective ear to say, "OK, Barry, you're driving us all crazy; now can we please move on!"

If you'll be providing tape for the session, purchase it now. At the time of this writing, there were only two analog tape suppliers left, and one of them (Quantegy) held about 90 percent of the market, so it should be easy to track down an outlet. But be sure to get tape that matches the engineer's exact specifications, down to the label and type. How much tape do you need? Twice as much as you think you'll need. When you run out of tape, everything comes to a halt. It's always better to have too much than not enough.

Here's a little horror story about tape from Patrick Ford:

One time I mixed a finished piece of product down at a real nice 24-track studio—weeks of work, finished thang, down onto the half-inch, final mix. It was done on analog. Then I took that tape with me to get it mastered. And when we started working on it, something sounded real strange right from the git-go. Pretty soon we began to realize that the tape wasn't balanced properly. We were getting a lot more out of one side than the other side. It ends up that this whole batch of tape that I had mixed to was no good. It had deteriorated. None of this half-inch tape held up. It all began to break down soon after we used it. It looked like I was going to have to remix the entire project, so the tape company flew a guy up to try and save it. Now, that's something that you can't avoid. But you have to know that these things can happen. When it comes to recording, make sure you go in with more tape than you're ever going to need.

If you're recording ensemble, prepare a setup chart that shows who will be positioned where inside the studio. The setup chart should also list the specifics on the instruments that will be used—for example, guitar, acoustic; guitar, 12 string. And it should detail the drum kit. Get that chart and the tape into the hands of the engineer three days before going in.

ON THE DAY

On the day of the first session, check off everything from the list on your way out the door. When you load in at the studio, check everything off that list again. That may sound ridiculous, but if anything has been forgotten, broken, or lost along the way, the time to run out and get another one, find it, or fix it is before you get underway. If you discover one of these simple oversights later, it can put a dead stop to the session until it's resolved.

Usually you can get into the studio half an hour before your session. After you load in, place your instruments inside the studio proper so they can become acclimated to the studio temperature and humidity. Who knows how much frustration is caused by instruments needing this simple attention?

A sound tech is likely to be around setting up, and there will be someone in the control room. Don't bother them except to ask where you should set your instruments. If you have anything for the engineer, now's the time to hand it over. If you notice anything about the setup that's wrong (where the drummer is placed, the temperature of the room, lighting, mics), let it be known. Then disappear. Stick around but make yourself invisible.

If you're going in to do vocals—no grease in the old voice box four hours before the session. No chicken, no pizza, no milk product. Drink plenty of water before going into the studio.

POSTPRODUCTION SCHEDULING

I read somewhere that every hour of tracking translates into three hours in the mix. That sounds entirely possible. From my own experience recording an acoustic instrument solo, every hour in the studio translates into about half an hour messing around editing.

Strangely enough, a lot of that time is spent either explaining things to the engineer that you thought were understood, discovering things worked out differently on tape from what you'd expected, or negotiating over aesthetic decisions that the engineer insists should be made on a technical level. With more complicated music, three hours in the mix for every hour in the studio sounds entirely possible.

The *Musician's Guide to Independent Record Production* by Will Connelly (the only source I could find willing to offer such an estimate in print) tells us that "one-half hour of post-production studio time for each minute of releasable material is fairly conservative. Two hours of studio time per minute of material is fairly generous" (Chicago: Contemporary Books, 1981, p. 111). Calculating at that rate, you can expect to spend an hour and a half to six hours on each three-minute-long tune.

No one I interviewed felt comfortable offering a tracking to mix ratio (there are just too many factors, variables, and possibilities), but if you anticipate an hour of mixing for every two hours of tracking, you'll at least have something to go on for scheduling purposes. How many minutes of "releasable material" that translates into is another matter entirely. Again, it depends on how complicated your music is and how much tracking was done with the mix in mind. If you go in and just start filling up tracks—a very common mistake—the mix could take forever. When that final trumpet blows, the moon turns as red as blood, and the night sky rolls up like scorched sack cloth, you'll still be at the board mixing.

This much we do know: if you've done your part in preproduction—all your tunes are routine before going in—and if things go down according to schedule in the studio, then the mix should go easily, if not quickly.

6

STUDIO
DECORUM

THE MOST ENTERTAINING reading in the tales of the rock band genre is recording studio horror stories. Pick up any book purporting to delineate the history of a band, and amid the lurid lies you'll find at least one painfully true story about lifelong buddies going at it toe-to-toe in the studio while in the booth the weary engineer looks on slack-jawed and bug-eyed and the drummer goes stomping out of the studio, threatening never to return again. There is something about the recording studio that can make otherwise rational beings lose their composure, their dignity, and their sanity. If you're a band, the process is almost guaranteed either to bond you together permanently or to tear you irreparably asunder.

Of course, the potential for such high melodrama is minimized when everyone respects the position and the task of everyone else involved in the project. It's minimized further if everyone recognizes that the studio is a place to do work and that, in order to get some work done, a certain amount of etiquette must be in place. Common courtesy is the key.

EXPECTATIONS OF THE STUDIO STAFF

The studio staff expects the artist to be there for the same reason they are there—to get some work done. So be professional. Be on time. Be ready to play. Be casual but be cooperative. Arriving unprepared, arriving without equipment, arriving late, arriving drunk, not arriving at all, or disappearing during tracking are all uncalled for.

Apparently, upstart musicians do more than their share of grumbling, both in the studio and after the fact. That's what I'm told. But it's not the wise thing to do. To a surprising degree, what the engineer thinks of the artist—not as an artist but personally—*can* have a lot to do with the results. If the engineer likes you, you'll get a little extra consideration. Most people are willing to go out of their way a bit to accommodate someone they like. On the other hand, an engineer who forms a bad opinion of you is just going to want to get the project over with.

Some even take it a step further. I've been told of cases in which engineers embedded socially unacceptable noises in songs simply because they didn't like the person they were working with. Poison in jest. Naturally, that's not going to happen if the engineer respects you or has empathy for you.

The manner in which you conduct yourself immediately upon arrival at the studio may well set the tone for sessions throughout the project. If you start out right, you'll have a good chance to establish a good working situation. So arrive on time, ready to play.

Admittedly and understandably, most musicians going into the studio for the first time are a bit nervous. For some the experience is downright scary. There are stories about musicians who were so nervous in the studio that they dropped their instruments; there are stories about singers rendered incapable of croaking so much as a single note. There are tales about people breaking down in tears. But I've never known a singer who wouldn't belt out a tune at the drop of a hat (even if the hat was dropped by accident). And no one I've quizzed can recall ever having seen a musician drop an instrument (smashing it intentionally is another matter). It's difficult to imagine anyone that nervous. And tears are properly reserved for beauty pageants.

Nevertheless, nervousness in the studio is common. What's nice is that it's also understood. If you're nervous, everyone on the staff will be sympathetic and will try to help you work through it. Being nervous is both understandable and acceptable. Serious problems arise, however, when musicians overcompensate for their nervousness by making peculiar attempts to impress the studio staff.

The two classic approaches are "Oh, I have a little project studio at home, so I know all about this" and "I'm so good I'll come in really wrecked and still blow you away."

The first approach—which usually involves spouting a lot of terminology and studio jargon—doesn't accomplish anything. Unless you hold an advanced degree in gate and peak limitations or have penned the definitive tome on ducking and keying, repeating something cool one of your buddies once said about phantom power isn't going to impress anyone. Making ridiculous statements that are anathema to the engineer only establishes the limits of your knowledge.

As in many aspects of life, the people who know the most are also the least likely to put their knowledge on display. On the other hand, people who have a recently acquired, limited grasp of a few particulars are always eagerly looking for an opportunity to spew forth a rhapsody of wisdom. But in the studio, whatever you may know (or pretend to know) is weighed against your performance. Your involvement in anything beyond your performance will probably be seen as nothing more or less than getting underfoot.

Just to be clear, though, I'm not saying that you shouldn't ask questions. The artist needs the assurance that asking questions provides. Whatever other dread illusions you may suffer under, don't be afraid to ask questions. Asking questions of people who know what they're talking about is the wise thing to do. There is knowledge in the studio—whoever is seated at the console has the knowledge—so take advantage of it. Get what you can. The president of a major label, a man who has produced over 150 albums, advises, "Don't be afraid to sound stupid. I ask stupid questions all the time."

Dale Miller concurs:

> Don't be ashamed to admit that you don't know something. Unless somebody's really a jerk, they're not going to be upset if you say, "I'm sorry, I don't know what that means." I think the only time you run into trouble is when you're so concerned about being hip that you don't tell them when you don't understand. When they start talking about dBs and roll-offs and stuff—I don't understand that stuff too much myself and I've had a reasonable amount of studio experience. But I'm never afraid to tell a guy, "Hey, man, I don't know what you're talking about." You know, I just say, "I want the guitar to sound warmer. I want the guitar to sound brighter. I want more bottom. I want more top end." I talk in those terms. And if someone starts talking about roll-off above ten billion kila-joules, I just say, "Hey, I honestly do not know what the hell you're talking about."

The second approach—getting loaded and loud—doesn't work because it's been done so many wearisome times before that most studio personnel, given the option, would rather attempt to extract their own wisdom teeth, in the dark, wearing mittens, using only vise grips and pot shards, than suffer through yet one more childish display of that sort. Getting loaded only makes you look bad and play badly.

Of course, we can always count on Frank Zappa to put things into perspective. Here's what he had to say about this matter: "A drug is neither moral nor immoral—it's just a chemical compound. The compound itself is not a menace to society until a human being treats it as if its consumption bestows a temporary license to act like an asshole."

The studio staff has certain expectations of artists, and none of them include drugs, drunkenness, stupidity, or arrogance. Whatever you may see on Empty-V, such nonsense has no place in the studio, and it's never welcome. In the studio a little humility goes a long way. The good news is, *you're not there to impress anyone anyway.*

If you want to really impress people in the studio, it's simple. Come in, sit down, tune up, do a run-through or two. Be patient and cooperative during testing. Wait quietly until the engineer cues you. When you hear, "Rolling," close your eyes, take a deep breath, and just nail it. There's nothing more impressive than going in and simply doing what you're in there to do. It's more impressive than anything else you might contrive. This is the way session players handle their job, and no one in the industry gets greater respect. Some session players are paid a lot better than most recording artists (and it's all fee work). Come in, do your work.

PERFORMANCE

Musicians who have trained as stage performers may feel a bit lost in the studio because what matters playing live and what matters playing in the studio are different. As said before, everything the artist may rely upon in performance—spontaneity, improvisation, audience response, accompaniment, the ability to move around, showmanship, and other factors that feed life into live performance—are all purposefully, necessarily, and strictly absent in the recording studio.

For bands tracking any portion of their tunes solo, the ongoing communication that keeps the band together on stage will be gone. In the studio you may find yourself lost if you're used to seeing Big Bones cue you with a nod of his head before you downshift into that slow shuffle, because Bones won't be there. In a situation like that, you may be having difficulty and not even know why. What you're used to doing on stage is largely unconscious; in the studio it all becomes conscious.

If showmanship is an integral part of your ability to perform and audience response a large part of your motivation, the restrictions of studio work can be deflating and possibly even a bit oppressive. There's almost no room for showmanship while tracking—your position in relationship to a fixed mic is usually critical—and studio personnel are not there in lieu of an audience.

On top of that, when studio personnel respond at all to a take, they may sound cold, unenthusiastic, and flat. This is partly due to the fact that their reaction is coming to you through the talkback, but it's also due to the fact that the people in the booth are being paid to remain analytical. If they're good, they're probably preoccupied with their tasks. Objectivity requires some distancing. So if they come across as indifferent, it may mean nothing more than they're doing their jobs. They're staying focused; they're working.

When an engineer says a take is "good," that simply means it was recorded successfully. The engineer is there not to judge the aesthetics of your performance but rather to evaluate the successfulness of the recording. Most critical comment from the booth has to do *only* with capturing the sound. That's really all you want from the engineer. As a performer, if you need more, look to your producer to provide it.

The combination of restricted performance and the absence of an enthused audience may, in fact, be the real cause behind the childish petulance some performers display in the studio. But who cares? Whatever the reason for it, such action doesn't accomplish anything and it's not welcome in the studio. The age-old wisdom stands: take your work seriously, but don't take yourself too seriously. Leave your ego at the door. If TAFKAP can do it, anyone can.

Charlie Musselwhite advises: "Don't let your ego get in the way of the project. And don't tolerate somebody else's bullshit either. Don't be afraid to eject somebody from the studio, even if you have to end the session for the day or delay things until you can get somebody else to take their place. I don't ever tolerate stuff like that. Nobody should *ever* be allowed to disrupt the session."

The other side of that coin is that sometimes the project is taken just a bit *too* seriously by the artist. Consequently, musicians sometimes find themselves working under enormous self-imposed pressure. Guitarist Christine Lakeland, in a 1990 *Bay Blues* interview, offered some healthy insight into that matter. She told me, "You know, I look at making recordings as kind of a bookmark. You do it and, after . . . you'll always think of what you *could have done* better . . . you find yourself listening only to the mistakes . . . but you have to finish it and move on. Because, six months or a year later you'll sound different anyway. You gotta get it done and keep goin'."

I've heard this same enlightened attitude expressed by other artists as well. It doesn't mean that these artists do not take their work in the studio seriously. It only means that they keep it in perspective. Whether this is your first time going in or not, it might be helpful to bear in mind that it won't be your last. You'll have another shot at it, and next time you'll have a little experience under your belt.

"WHAT'S TAKING SO LONG?"

Studio professionals tell us that artists are continually whining about how much time the recording process takes. Typically, musicians see any time that they are not grinding out their music as a waste of time. In actuality, most of what artists perceive as a waste of time is spent making the adjustments necessary to the task of getting a good recording. If you've done recording at home, then you probably recognize reasonable on-site preparation, testing, and adjustments for what they really are—requisite to getting a professional, commercially viable sound.

First-timers are sometimes simply unfamiliar with how much time things may take in the studio. Even a simple task, like rolling back the tape, can seem to take an unusually long time if you've had no experience with it. Trying to minimize leakage between the cymbals and bass drum, bass drum and toms, may seem to take forever (especially when overhead mics are used), but it isn't a waste of time. Any time spent micing an instrument or adjusting levels or listening to playback is spent for your benefit.

There are many times during tracking when nothing appears to be happening at all. The artist is stranded in the studio, with no indication of what's going on, and there's nothing but silence from the booth. At such times the artist—with no other information—may feel that time is just being wasted. But "delays" that occur while the engineer corrects a problem are not, as some musicians perceive them, a waste of time. Correcting technical problems is necessary for the success of the project. It might help to remember that the engineer is not the cause of a problem but merely the person who detects and corrects it. The engineer actually keeps you from really wasting your time by playing a stratospheric solo into a dead mic.

Too many artists—both first-timers and experienced recording artists—use any break in the action as a cue to clown around or wander off somewhere without letting anyone know where to find them or when they might be expected to reappear. An enlightened way to spend your time during any delay is to do a run-through or just sit and regain your composure. Prepare yourself for the next take. In other words, stay focused on your work.

The worst waste of time is leaving the studio between takes to go into the booth and just hang out.

WHO'S THE BOSS?

The recording studio is a place of business. More importantly to you, it's a place to get your work done. In order to get any real work done, a certain reasonable decorum is expected. Expected but never enforced. Although the studio staff is not there to babysit you, to laugh at your jokes, to make runs to the liquor store for you, or to host your private party, most of them will do these things as long as you pay them good money to do so. If you plan to treat studio sessions like a party, there are much cheaper ways to throw a party. It's your money and your time.

Maybe it's from watching too many rock videos, but some musicians go into the studio as if they owned the place. Admittedly, the staff *are* all hired hands. However, you'll get along better and get better results from your efforts if you recognize the simple, undeniable fact that *they* are in the driver's seat. After all, they own and operate all the equipment; they know how to accomplish the task at hand. They're the ones with the experience. Respect their position. Some artists feel that by stepping into the studio they've passed into a world where all rules are suspended. It's not true.

Respect their workplace. If you've got to carry on, stay in the lobby. If you absolutely need to do certain things (drink, smoke dope, have friends in, horse around), do them in a part of the building where they won't interfere with other people's work. Think about it from the engineer's perspective. He or she is in the booth, carefully trying to monitor sound, when a couple of guys wander in, yammering loudly, carrying pizza and beer and cigarettes. Is that the best atmosphere for this professional to be in while working on your project?

Although studio personnel may be in the position to offer good advice, they won't foist it upon you. Generally, they won't go against your will either. In most cases, whenever there is a conflict, they'll simply back off and grant the client's wishes. For example, as far as running your session is concerned, they won't step in to keep you from blowing your entire budget fooling around with the basic tracks. And as far as common sense is concerned, they may or may not call for an ambulance when you overdose in the bathroom. Usually all they really want is for the session to remain both professional and friendly. If they can't get professional, they'll settle for friendly.

When it comes to confrontation, the studio staff usually demurs quietly. When it comes to client demands, they usually surrender—even if they know what's best. Consequently, people who clearly do not know what they're doing sometimes end up sitting at the board, making decisions that could ruin a project. If your uncle Bob has always wanted to fly one of the big boards, and you, as the client, give him the nod, the studio staff isn't going to ride herd on your unbridled stupidity.

Behind the scenes, within the fraternity of recording studio professionals, stories about dullards commandeering the console offer endless entertainment. Some guy comes in, takes over the board, and sits there furiously twisting knobs and barking orders—like the captain of the *Titanic* shortly after striking the iceberg—but the only problem is, he's twisting all the wrong knobs.

We're told that some studios have a bank of faders—replete with nicely lit, brightly colored buttons and meters—that are responsive but not active. Needles move, lights glow, but they're not attached to anything. They're just there, on one end of the console, to accommodate self-appointed buffoons. With this prop in place, the real work can continue while the commander sits at the board—like the baby in the car seat with the big yellow plastic steering wheel. Honk honk, look at me, I'm drivin'!

Engineers have also been known to quietly set aside the tape when such clients come into the booth. Then they can sit back, unconcerned, and let the hotshots do whatever they've got to do in order to feel like they're contributing. After that's all out of the way, the engineer simply hands over the tape that was set aside. Although the tape is unaltered in any way, the client usually hears a remarkable improvement after supposedly applying a touch of genius to the project. Amazingly, such clients are almost never run out of the booth with a loaded shotgun or horse-laughed right out of the studio. On the contrary, some get producer's credits on the label.

THE ARTIST AS KING

Renting studio time does not confer a position of royalty, and the staff is not the artist's personal servants. But you would think so if you observed some of what goes on in the studio.

Charlie Musselwhite tells us:

I hear about these bands that go into the studio and they have this attitude; they like to scream at people. They boss people around and act like prima donnas. Boy, I have *no* use for people like that. I mean, life is too short. People that act like that should really be in some other business.

I can understand losing your temper or getting up tight about somebody not pulling their weight and hindering the project, but you shouldn't be in there creating tension and anxiety because of your own ego trip. And that happens a lot. That happens even in clubs. People go into a club and right away start giving the sound man a hard time. But that's really stupid, because people talk about that stuff. You shouldn't think that just because there's nobody there—it's only you and the band and the sound engineer, and you're screaming at him—that nobody's gonna hear about it. You know, all those guys, those sound guys, talk to each other. Like, "Oh yeah, *that* guy. I wouldn't ever work for him again!"

The person who caused the scene will go somewhere and, they won't know it, but the people behind the scenes, the engineers and all, will be prepared: "Oh yeah, this idiot!" A bad attitude has been established even before they get there.

If you've had a problem someplace before, and you're slated to go there again, Charlie recommends:

When you get there next time, straighten things out. Go up right away and say, "You know, last time I was here . . . I don't know what you heard, but my side of it is . . . . Just to get things straight." Because people, when they tell these things, they always report it in their own favor.

You want *everybody* to like your project and to like your music. And even if they don't like your project and don't understand your music, you at least want them to like you as a person so that they'll work for you and try to get down on tape what it is you're trying to do. You shouldn't be in there making enemies. These people, if they like you, are gonna try to help you. So you should feel good about what they're doing and you should appreciate what they're doing.

As a general rule, when dealing with *anyone* in the music community, be nice. Treat everybody in a kind manner; after all, they just might be everything they pretend to be. And even those who aren't still have the ability to talk. Years ago someone gave me some advice that has served me pretty well as an interviewer. So I'll pass it on. Treat every small guy as if he might be a big guy; treat every big guy as if he might be just another guy. From my experience, this works. But it *only* works in a work situation. If you approach Otis Rush backstage with credentials, it works nicely. If you approach Graham Nash in a grocery store checkout line in Felton, you can expect a cold, aristocratic, "Do I *know* you?"

ALCOHOL

The Buddha observed that intoxicating drink causes stupidity and therefore should be avoided. But it doesn't take a wise person to observe the part that alcohol and drugs play in the music scene. Of course, there are some very good reasons why musicians turn to drugs or alcohol, but that doesn't make these habits any less costly. It's just unfortunate that those who have these habits drag it out for so many years and drag so many good people down with them as they go.

It's really a very simple matter. Each artist has to decide what his or her goals are and what to do in order to accomplish those goals. If your goal is to become a thorn in the sides of the people you work with and never-ending heartbreak for those who care about you, that's easily done. If your goal is to be the best musician you can be, that might demand a little more from you.

If you're going to use alcohol like a loaded gun aimed at your career, here's a story that will give you all the ammunition you might ever need. It's about one of the most incredible performances ever delivered . . . by an alcoholic.

At the 1966 Newport Folk Festival, Alan Lomax constructed a stage setting to look like a Mississippi juke joint, stocked it with whiskey, put Howlin' Wolf and Booker White and Skip James and Son House in there, and just let the camera roll while what went on went on. And what went on, of course, was a lot of really good, good-time blues. After Skip James, it wasn't long before Booker White got 'em all up and dancin'.

Then Son House, who'd apparently been drinking, sat down and offered up one of the most heart-rending performances ever captured on video. It was an incredible, torturous version of "Forever on My Mind."

The delivery was ungainly. It was clearly the work of a man either too old or too drunk to play. It was all out of time. The plodding beat was reinstated, always at the very last possible moment, with a heavy hand slamming down defiantly through the strings. At the same time, it was a deeply profound performance. The plaintive words of the song seemed torn, unaltered, directly from the man's soul. This is not hyperbole. The lure of it was inescapable. The small gathering, which only seconds earlier had been laughing, dancing like fools and carrying on loudly, were now, every single one of them, silent, penitent. Their eyes were riveted solemnly on Son House.

Near the end of the tune, you could see the old man's mind at work, trying to recall where it was headed and how to finish up. But that only added to the impact when, after some apparent confusion, he wrapped it up decisively. Then Son House leaned forward in his chair, rested one arm on his guitar, and looked around calmly at the crowd as if to explain, "That's everything I have to say." It was a powerful, painful, absolutely unforgettable performance.*

The only thing that could possibly have proven more powerful than that performance was the seemingly un-called-for, viciously personal attack on Son House that occurred later.

When it came time for his set, Howlin' Wolf began with a long, spoken introduction about what the blues is and who has the blues. He said, "[When] in your heart you feel that you ain't nobody, then you got the blues." Wolf pointed over

---

* The Son House performance I've described here can be found on *Devil Got My Woman: Blues at Newport 1966*, Vestapol 13049, a videotape from Stefan Grossman's Guitar Workshop, Inc., (201) 729-5544. Call and they'll send you a free 64-page catalog.

at Son House. "See, this man here got the blues. Right there. That's where the blues comes from. See. He done drunk up all of his . . . and he's worried."

Son House started to offer a good-natured defense from across the room: "But the nice thing about it is . . ." But Wolf stepped up his assault, cutting Son House short. "See, you had a chance with your life, and you ain't done nothin' with it. So you got to have the blues." Son House tried to defend himself by saying something about women. But Wolf wasn't letting him off the hook. "We ain't talkin' about the womens; we're talkin' about the life of a human being, how they live it. See, now you don't love but one thang and that's whiskey . . . and that's plumb out of it."

The question, What would that performance have been like if Son House had been sober? is beside the point. Anyone who's going to drink or do drugs is going to drink or do drugs, and as anyone who has tried knows, there ain't nothing anyone can do to stop them. But it's not just one performance we're talking about. Wolf had it right. "We're talkin' about *the life of a human being,* how they live it." That's the final word.

SOME BASIC RULES FOR BANDS

If you're working with a band, control your own people.

Share the risk. Do not let any single person financially back the project. If everybody's invested, everybody's going to do what they can to get the project done.

Try to remain open to other's suggestions. Everybody should feel comfortable enough to talk and exchange ideas.

Don't get angry if your idea or suggestion isn't used.

Try to keep a feeling of camaraderie. "Let's have some fun here." Try not to let it get out of hand.

No wives, husbands, girlfriends, boyfriends, lovers, kids, or pets. Their presence is a distraction. For other musicians who may not know them, it can be inhibiting. If you'd like someone around, ask your fellow musicians if that will be OK with them. Although you do not need their approval, you might also ask the studio staff.

Leave the booze and weed at home. If you're ill prepared musically, drinking the whole day and trying to perform drunk will usually be exposed in playback as a monumentally flawed approach.

Generally, there's no smoking in the booth. No food in the booth.

No conversation in the booth about anything other than what's going on in the booth, unless the engineer initiates it.

Establish a chain of command. Get everybody to recognize and accept it.

Agree beforehand to go by your producer's decisions about when to quit, when to take a break, when to do another take, and when a take is adequate.

Allow your producer to look after your best interests in the control room. Make sure, before going in, that your producer understands what you're after and knows how to go about achieving it. Then let the producer do the job.

Inform the studio of any changes in the schedule. If the studio is expecting to mix and you show up wanting to retake the guitar solo, the switch will require setting up, micing, and adjusting levels—all of which take time—*your* time—time you could be tracking.

Respect the expertise of the people you're working with.

If you're given a direct phone number into the booth, do not call that number unless it's absolutely necessary, and only if you can't reach anyone by any other method. The person who picks up that line is probably working. Be respectful of his or her time.

If there's a problem with the engineer, wait for an appropriate moment to make your point known. Remember, there are reasons something may sound not quite right to you. Wait until the engineer has made any adjustments and offers you a playback. If you still have doubts, ask.

When dealing with studio personnel, ask questions; do not give commands. There is a big difference between asking them to do something for you and telling them what to do. Ultimately, the difference may affect not just how much work gets done but also the quality of the final product.

Communicate your needs in your usual language. Avoid studio jargon. If you have questions, cast them in your normal language.

Unless invited into the booth, your place is in the studio. No matter how much you may know or how helpful you want to be, stay out of the booth.

Wait quietly between takes. Occupy your time while waiting by focusing on the project.

If you screw up, don't kick yourself. It's part of the process. *Everyone* makes mistakes. Everybody has a bad day once in a while. The perfect take is an extreme rarity.

No backbiting during breaks. If things are going kind of rough, attacking each other during the break is not going to improve anything. If you have to walk away in order to keep your mouth shut, walk away.

Work out all arguments before or after the session, outside the studio. Otherwise, you're paying studio time while you debate these matters.

If you are not working on a particular session, stay away from the studio. Ask your producer for a copy of the rough mix of the session if it affects your own work. But if you're not slated to play, stay away.

"Never leave the mother ship." Stay with the project. If you do wander off during the session, let someone know where you're going and, if possible, when to expect to see your lovely face again.

If you've got to make a phone call or something like that, try to time it so that it doesn't disrupt the flow of the session.

Don't ever duct-tape anything in the studio.

AND FINALLY . . .

If things are going well in the studio—or if things got a little bit wacky for a while and you've gotten back on track—take the time to say thanks. Before you pick up the last bag to load out, step into the booth and say, "Hey, thanks for helping us out. Things are going really well. We appreciate it."

7

....

TRACKING

....

I N THE STUDIO the difference between professionals and first-timers is that the professionals have probably (finally) surrendered to the undeniable, unassailable fact that things in the studio take time. Maybe they've given in willingly, or maybe they've been beaten into submission by experience, but when professional recording artists go into the studio, they have already decided to live with that fact. Things in the studio take time. Some things take a lot of time.

Recording can be exciting, boring, fulfilling, strenuous, wonderful, demanding, unforgiving, freeing, better than sex, your worst nightmare, and somehow, both endless and over too soon. No one will ever say it isn't worth it.

They've also developed skills necessary for dealing with the studio process, among them skills for handling tedium, handling repetition, handling down time while other necessary tasks are performed, handling frustration. They've learned to be flexible, reliable, and to plan ahead. More important, they've learned how to pace themselves, when to take a break, how to listen to their own music critically, and how to work with other professionals. With all that in mind let's consider:

TAKES AND RETAKES

Professionals know that if it takes a thousand takes, then it takes a thousand takes. Although they try to get the best possible take right out of the box, they know from experience that it's unlikely. Whatever level you're at (from the artist's POV), doing takes *is* the recording process.

Doing takes and retakes is not merely *part of* the recording process; it is the process itself. Tedium and screw-ups are merely *part of* the process.

Professional musicians do multiple takes in order to have as many takes as possible to choose from. The amateur may do multiple takes in an effort to get one good, usable take (or enough pieces to stitch one together). Doing 50 takes of each four-bar section and then mixing from there, as Frank Zappa was known to do, sounds like it could only lead to the worst possible editing nightmare imaginable, but the point is clear. If you're not ready or willing or able to hack your way through the same tune a dozen times—each time aiming at renewed perfection—then you're probably not ready, willing. or able to go into the studio. Tracking requires a certain complacency of demeanor.

Listen critically to playbacks. Doing retakes while you're still tracking is easier than editing and certainly less costly than setting up again. So professional musicians always take the time to listen carefully to each playback. That's an important part of the process. First-timers (and others, too), in an effort to get things done quickly, sometimes take this part of the process too lightly, only to find out later that they can't live with the results.

GETTING IT IN ONE SHOT

Tales about going into the studio and cutting a tune in one shot are, for all intents and purposes, myths. Nothing more. And such myths do more harm than good. Believing in myths only sets you up for disappointment.

It's important that you don't start questioning your ability to produce simply because you can't nail a tune on the first take. In soloing, doing a dozen takes or two dozen takes is not unusual at all. In ensemble work you can reasonably expect the basic tracks for a tune to fill up the entire first session and, more likely than not, spill over into a second. Harmonies and vocals typically take more time than the basic tracks. Expect it.

WHEN YOU ARRIVE

The idea that you will arrive, go in, set up, and begin to play is an all-too-common misunderstanding. When you arrive, the engineer will have already prepared for your arrival, doing things in advance to make the session go smoothly: cleaned up after the preceding session, organizing cords, mics, and miscellany; checked the studio equipment to be sure it's all in working order, cleaning and demagnetizing the recording heads (work done before each session); and made sure the board is set up—dialed in on settings that might have been established during previous sessions—establishing the track assignments for each line in. When you arrive, the engineer should be ready to start working with you.

In the studio, stools should be in position, headphones in place, baffles established. The selection and general positioning of the mics will have been taken care of. In short, the studio will be set up according to the musicians who'll be playing that session and for the instruments they'll be using. It will look like it's ready to go. But that doesn't mean you are ready to go.

When you go into the studio, your personal position within the studio will be prearranged (according to your setup chart if you've supplied one). You'll also be told where to set up amps, drums, or other equipment, depending upon the requirements of the room.

The staff will try to accommodate any special considerations you may have. For example, guys who are used to playing together on stage may need to have line-of-sight contact. If you have any such considerations, make them known.

If you're tracking solo, the absence of the others from the room may be disconcerting. You may feel abandoned. Take comfort in the fact that almost everyone feels that way going in. Many times, as a performer, you'll have to deliver whether you feel like performing or not. Consider this just another one of those situations. Be as professional as possible. Think about why you're there. Take a deep breath, employ any methods you might normally use to quash stage fright, and just give it your best.

When it comes to getting a good take, being comfortable may be a larger factor than most people might guess. You have to be as comfortable as possible. If you can't work where they've put you or you can't work solo, speak up. With some artists, soloing just doesn't work. If you're used to working with the band and they want to isolate you, ask to be placed in a room without the headphones but with the big speakers cranked up. That way you'll get closer to the sounds you're used to and you'll be able to move around a bit.

Be aware that the studio takes getting used to. The reason the staff asks that you try working one way or another is that it will deliver superior results. So give their way an honest try before you give up. If there's something that can be done to make it work, let your needs be known.

Vocalists, I'm told, are notorious for remaining quiet about what they need in order to perform. But it's important to speak up. If you want the headphones off, say so. If you want the room colder or warmer or lighter or darker, or if you want candles or you need to see someone special in the booth while you sing, say so. If there's anyone around who makes you nervous, say so. If you are more comfortable recording with your back turned or standing or sitting, say so. If anything might lead to a better take and the studio staff can accommodate you, they will.

Anytime you have questions about what's going on, address your questions to your producer. If you can't rely on the producer's expertise, at least rely on the fact that he or she is on your side.

MICROPHONES

The right microphones are an extremely important part of getting what you want on tape. A dozen mics placed precisely in the same position will give you a dozen different results. That's why selection is crucial. When you hear a recording that's done in a studio with mega-stars, you're hearing microphones that cost thousands of dollars each. When you go into an average, run-of-the-mill studio, you'll probably be using microphones that cost hundreds of dollars each. The difference between the two *is* noticeable, even to the untrained ear. Microphones are certainly one of those areas where you get what you pay for.

There are literally hundreds of mics to choose from. Each is built with a specific use in mind. They are classified according to the method they use to pick up sound, the pattern and size of the area in which they can pick up sound, the dynamic range they cover, whether they are driven or passive, high impedance or low, and how much of the sound they pick up is passed on. Mics are selected not only for their ability to pick up sounds you want to record but also for their *inability* to pick up sounds you do not want to record. On top of all that, selection of the right microphone is undeniably also an aesthetic decision, because microphones add something of their own to the mix (referred to as color). Clearly, selection alone is a complex and crucial matter.

Any sound technician will tell you that placement is as important as the microphone itself. When you place a microphone, you're micing not only the instrument but, in effect, the entire room (this is called *room feel*).

There are dozens of micing techniques. The most common is close micing. In close micing the mic is positioned to capture the sound directly from one source and thus ensure isolation. The angle of the microphone is as important as its proximity to the source, since the frequency response varies according to the microphone's angle. So the difference between a good sound and a lousy sound may be adjustments as fine as 1/4 inch. Getting the placement right is a matter of experience and educated guesswork, followed up, of course, by testing. We're told that with the correct microphone placed correctly there is no need for equalization.

Air actually changes sound. And many frequencies need to travel some distance to develop. So in some instances microphones placed too close can generate their own problems. Additionally, things like the type of cable, the condition of the cable, the way it lies along the floor, and how the jack seats in the receptacle can have tremendous effects on a microphone.

Good microphones are more sensitive than you might suppose. Open mics can pick up radio frequency interference from the headphones of someone setting up in another room. And every microphone has the uncanny ability to pick up every sound you may not want picked up while, occasionally, refusing to pick up sounds you do want (a matter for EQ).

That's why microphone selection and placement are left up to the studio staff. They know which mics work best with the frequency range of the instruments you're taping. If they really know their stuff, they can look at the frequency response wave pattern of any particular mic, and talk knowingly about how it might compare with other mics. Even if you consider yourself a microphone expert, *listen to the results* achieved by the selection and placement the studio staff offers.

Initially, all you may need to know is that omni-directional mics pick up sound from all directions. The cardioid pattern is more focused and more flexible. Generally, if you want a more ambient sound, you simply move the mic back from the source. To isolate the sound a bit more, move it closer. Stereo mics pick up sounds from opposite directions and keep them separate. More than that will come from your personal studio experience.

TESTING

During testing, the engineer may ask you to get comfortable first, and then come into the studio to adjust the microphones' position accordingly. Microphones may be adjusted, readjusted, adjusted again. After all that, mics may be switched out. You may be asked to rearrange your position to the mic, but if the mic itself needs moving, a technician or the engineer will appear in order to do that. Do not ever touch a microphone unless you're asked to do so.

Once your position is set, they'll get you plugged in, hand you a headset, and abandon you for the control room. Take this opportunity to tune your instrument, go over the song in your mind and begin your run-throughs. Once the headphones are on, everything may take on a kind of strange quality. The headphones can make almost everything seem different.

Before anything gets on tape, levels must be set and the engineer will take some time to establish "alignment tones" at the beginning of the tape. Later, in mastering, these tones will be matched to guarantee an accurate reproduction.

Testing may be your first real opportunity to surrender to the expertise of the recording studio professionals you've hired. It might also be the first opportunity to practice patience. Testing includes the tuning of each instrument to concert pitch, with assistance and guidance from the engineer. You'll be asked to play very low. Then very loud. You may be asked to stop or to continue playing for some length of time without stopping. After making some adjustments, the engineer will probably ask you to go through all these steps again. Then the process will be repeated for each instrument involved in the session.

All the while the engineer is adjusting levels and looking for possible problems. Setting levels initially includes establishing gain (amplitude) and EQ for each line in. Gain, in general, is set to capture as much sound as possible without distortion. The EQ is adjusted to focus in on (enhance or emphasize) desired tones and to eliminate signals from other sources as well.

Typically, you'll do several run-throughs and find yourself sitting around waiting while the engineer rolls back tape and checks each channel for problems. The engineer is listening for the need for limiters, compression, or signal processing, and whether there are any problems with your instrument or technique that might affect the recording. At this point, the engineer is also establishing the session log—a record of track assignments, EQ settings, and takes. Throughout each session such notes are kept in order to help in setup for subsequent sessions.

If you're recording ensemble, the engineer will work with one instrument until the playback is satisfactory. For the basic tracks, the engineer will first help the drummer tune the drums and suggest whether to use dampening rings to deaden the tone. Mics will be adjusted. Then, starting with the bass, snare, and toms, the engineer will establish the EQ and the levels of each channel going to the tape machine. After those are set, the drummer will be asked to go into the booth and listen to the playback to see what kinds of changes might be needed. With the drummer back in the studio, the engineer will work on the cue level going to the drummer's headphones.

From there, it's on to the bass, establishing EQ and levels. The engineer will establish the headphone levels between the two so that they're in contact with each other. Add in the guitars; get their headphones set up. At each point, every instrument and every line in, the EQ and level are established, one at a time. After everybody's happy with their headphones, the engineer may try to get a feel for the tune while listening to each instrument during a run-through.

All of this may seem to take an unusually long time, but it's requisite to the task. During this process, simply do what you're asked to do. Don't worry, be happy. Before you know it, you'll be on your way.

After the engineer has established the levels on each instrument, you might want to go into the control booth and give a listen to what has been established. Listen to each track separately. You're in there not only to be sure you like the sound you're hearing, but also to listen for problems, like leakage between tracks. If you detect any problems that you think the engineer or producer may have overlooked, speak up. It's important that you do so. If you don't like what you're hearing, ask for an explanation before making demands. Re-emphasize what you're after. If you still have any doubts about whether they understand you or not, straighten out the producer.

It is usually at this point that the difference between the engineer's perspective and the artist's may become vitally clear for the first time. Of course, when you sit behind any instrument (or hold it in your hands), you hear it differently from the way others, out front, hear it. The sound of your instrument isolated and cleanly recorded and coming through headphones is bound to be different from what you're accustomed to hearing. You can anticipate that happening. Also, the engineer needs certain levels to record properly and to allow for some room to move in the mix. But you do not have to hear everything that the booth needs to hear. The engineer can adjust what you're hearing for your comfort.

THE CANS

Take the time to get a good mix in your headphones. The better you hear, the better you'll play. There's no reason to struggle with your offering if the solution is as simple as adjusting what you hear through the cans. The people in the booth have no way of knowing what you want, though, unless you make your needs known.

Tell the engineer how you would like your instrument to sound in your cans. They can be adjusted so you hear reverb on your instrument while tracking clean, for example. Explain what other instruments you need to hear in order to perform. If there is anything coming through your cans that you do not want to hear, if what you hear is disturbing to you in any way or making your job difficult, speak up. If you would like it quieter or louder, or if you'd like to hear more bass or you want some channel cut out entirely, say so, and the engineer will do whatever is possible.

Not everybody can, or will, work with headphones. I'm told of an old blues-man who was convinced that he'd be electrocuted by headphones. Some musicians refuse to use them because it gives them a false sense of what's going on. The headphones can certainly make you feel uncertain about what's being played and what's going on tape. If you're used to playing live, an alternative is to set up in the same room with your amplifier and keep one ear uncovered. Keeping one ear uncovered is a fairly common approach. Hearing the mix and where you are live at the same time may give you a better feel for what's going on. If the headphones are creating a problem, you can play without them.

At any point while tracking—from this moment until the final mix—what you hear through your headphones may not be (for you) a good indication of what's being recorded. In the studio the music is isolated, segmented, recorded at very high gain with extreme fidelity, and played back as pure, unadulterated sound. The simple act of tuning can sound magnificent and strange. Your own instrument or voice coming through the headphones may sound like the most wonderful thing you've ever heard. Or it may sound unlike anything you've ever heard before. Either way, it can be disorienting and require some time to get used to. Give yourself the time to adjust.

Raw tracks offer a somewhat exaggerated view. Also, don't forget that you're getting that view through tiny speakers. What you're hearing is certainly not a good indication of how the results will ultimately sound. You can safely assume that the engineer has a greater insight into what's needed in order to attain the best mix down the road. For many problems, having the volume in your head-phones turned down can make a world of a difference.

REFERENCE VOCALS

Vocalists who are either accustomed to hearing their voice processed or simply prefer to hear it that way, *can* track clean and still get the processed vocals through the cans. If you track clean with reverb coming through the cans, you'll have to prepare yourself to hear the difference in playback. Your vocal coming back to you without reverb for the first time can be a startling demonstration of how good you really are. There are stories about artists who were so overwhelmed upon hearing themselves the first time in playback that they broke down in tears. You may be a bit more critical.

There's no reason to be critical of your *performance* when cutting reference vocals, however. The point of this vocal track is not performance but only estab-lishing the timing of the song. You're simply cueing the other musicians, estab-lishing the pace you'll want on the final cut. So sing softly, sing low, and save your vocal cords. You do not want to blow your voice out on a scratch vocal.

"OK, TAKE ONE . . ."

Eventually you'll be cued, someone will say "rolling," the slate will be marked ("Take one"), and you'll be underway. Even after all the testing and adjustments, the first take is kind of an experiment to find out if everything is working. If anything isn't, it should become clear at this point. Many times during testing or run-throughs, the artist unconsciously backs off a notch or two, so when actual tracking begins, things have changed considerably. Whatever the outcome of the first take, you may have to wait a bit until the engineer is ready for take two. When you hear, "Rolling, take two," your job is pretty simple. Close your eyes, take a deep breath, go to work.

You might do several takes before the engineer asks you if you'd like to hear what you've done. During playback you can expect to be surprised, once again, by what you hear. If it sounds good, it will only get better. And what sounds lousy to you may be merely a matter of adjustment. Don't be disheartened. Give yourself some time. After being in the studio for a hour or so, you will find, more likely than not, that the process begins to make a little more sense.

TAKES

During tracking, your producer's job becomes critical. The producer should be listening for wandering tempo, bad notes, thumps, noises, lip smacks, screeching of your fingers against the strings, flat notes, sniffing, or anything else you wouldn't want on the final recording. If you do not have a producer, it's your job to listen for such problems. But listen for them only on playback. While you're playing, it's impossible to judge. Listening for mistakes while playing can only screw things up for you.

While tracking, try not to let mistakes slow you down or haunt you once they're committed to tape. Screw-ups are the norm. Keep in mind that *parts* of takes may prove usable. Many mistakes can be edited out, electronically improved through processing, or otherwise fixed in the mix. You can also go back and punch in a better version while tracking. The decision about how to handle a flub may take some thought, and that thinking may be postponed until sometime later, after you've produced more tape.

As said before, some of the stuff that sounds absolutely terrible as it occurs turns out to be more than adequate on playback. Some of it turns out to be a miracle. You may find yourself thinking, "I don't even know how I did that (let alone *why* I did that), but it sure works." Whatever you think of a take, always get the advice of your producer. Ask the engineer for an opinion as well. That's why you've hired their unsympathetic ears. The engineer is there to capture your skills. The producer is there to offer objective, aesthetic critique and support.

If you don't like the way things are going but the engineer and the producer both assure you everything's all right, accept it as fact. An important part of their job is objectivity. They know what can (and what cannot) be done at the board, in editing, and in the mix to correct problems. When it comes to what is good enough to save, what to scrap, what can be edited out, and which parts from other takes may be edited in (at this stage of the game), rely on their expertise. If the advice from the booth is that a take is good enough, move on. The opposite is also true. If the word from the booth is that you need to take another shot at it, bow to their expertise.

Patrick Ford tells this story:

> I was working with a young band—it wasn't the kind of music that I normally would work with—they were playing some very hard-edge, contemporary stuff. And the lead singer, while he was very talented, had a hard time hitting the notes just right. He was the kind of guy who, given some training or another five years, would be a great singer. But for the present, he was not quite there.
>
> When we would finish a track, I'd say, "This is a good track, the energy's good, *but* we're gonna have to work on the vocal parts." And he'd come back at me with things like "Hey man, that's the way I wanted it to sound! I like that rawness!" which is just a cop-out for not accepting the fact that it could be done better. If the artist is in there to make the best possible product, their role is to listen to that producer. Because if they've got a good producer, that producer is in there to get a successful project, not just to fulfill the fantasies and feed the ego of one of the artists.

With things like vocals, sweetener, and key instrumental solos, you can't be too finicky. There are things, however, that you *can* be too finicky about.

It's important not to get so finicky with the bed tracks (the basic tracks/rhythm tracks) that you run out of studio time. This is a common mistake. Musicians get so involved in perfection at the outset that they end up rushing vocals in order to finish the project on time. Remember that basic tracks are, for the most part, usually masked by, if not entirely buried in, orchestration. On the other hand, they *are* the foundation on which the rest of the tune is constructed.

If you aren't satisfied with a take, inform the engineer, "I'd like to take another shot at that." The engineer may ask you if you want to save the preceding take. If there was anything good in it, you should. And the process begins again all over.

Bear in mind that the engineer is in the driver's seat when it comes to getting the recorded sound. This is the expert who knows what's needed, how the pieces will fit together, and what adjustments to make on each track before it finally comes together. That's the level on which the engineer makes decisions. If you have raging doubts, raise your questions quietly and with respect. For example, "The drums sound a little tinny right there. Is that gonna be corrected later?" It's important to trust in the engineer's ability.

As you add various effects or adjust the EQ, you affect the levels, so during tracking, the engineer continually monitors the signal and makes adjustments on each channel. While you're tracking, the engineer is looking for problems— channels that stick out and need adjusting down, channels that are too quiet and need adjusting up, sounds that are flat and may require tweaking, and so on. The addition of each new take potentially affects the mix. So the engineer is constantly revising settings, making adjustments, and taking notes.

With each take, the engineer learns a little bit more about the tune, the particular musician being recorded, the sound of the instrument, the position each track will take in the overall orchestration. If you've supplied a tape or a transcript of the tunes you plan to record, the engineer can anticipate (and therefore make appropriate adjustments for) passages as they come up. Without a tape or transcript, this familiarity can be gained only during tracking. It's something of an oversimplification to say that throughout the entire project, the engineer's job is one that demands complete, undivided attention.

"STAND BY"

Throughout the session, at any time, you may be told to stand by. It's possible that you won't hear anything from the engineer for several minutes. During this time, remain where you are, with your mind on what you're doing, and be ready to roll when they're ready in the control room. If it will help you to stay on track by playing, ask first. Decorum demands that you either ask or advise the people in the booth if what you intend to do has anything to do with making noise.

When the producer or engineer says, "Stand by," the silence from the booth can be almost oppressive. There's an awkwardness that comes with such silences, which engineers do not seem to be aware of, and generally no one is going to offer you an explanation. The engineer is focused on whatever task is at hand. Many times you won't be informed about what's going on because knowing that the engineer is considering feeding the signal directly from the sync heads to the key inputs in order to trigger the gate before the signal hits the repro head will not help you in any way in the studio. A good engineer will therefore purposely keep you out of what is going on so you can remain focused on your performance.

During such silences the artist, of course, is left guessing. It's not unusual to think, "Am I doing something wrong? Was it something I did that caused this delay?" But "delay" is the wrong word for what's going on. What's going on is merely the recording process. The recording process, if anything, is a process of continual adjustments. If the cause of the delay is something you're doing, they'll let you know.

The lighting in most studios is such that, in many situations, you may not be able to see clearly into the booth. On the other hand, the view from the booth into the studio is always clear and sharp. So you *know* they can see you. If the conversation in the booth is animated or the staff is laughing in there, it's easy to become paranoid. But the physical separation between the booth and the studio is not so they can talk about you behind your back. That separation is there to allow the artist and the engineer to maintain selective perspectives on the work at hand. Comfort yourself with the knowledge that during standby, the studio professionals are simply doing the work you're paying them to do.

Meanwhile, of course, your momentum has been halted, your concentration broken, and quite naturally you're anxious to get going again. By the time they're ready to go you could be a nervous wreck, if you allow that to happen. The solution is to set your worries aside. Stay focused on your task. Take the time to work out a difficult phrase or just practice. Stay limber. In the studio it's easy to forget what you're there for. There's a lot going on, and some of it is highly technical. Some of it's not technical at all but confusing nonetheless. The process is demanding, emotionally draining, and the ticking of the clock can be deafening. But if you remember what you're there for, it should be easier.

A good friend of mine, a remarkable blues guitarist named Carlos Guitarlos, used to hand out a business card that simply read: "Carlos Guitarlos, I'M HERE TO PLAY," with his phone number. The role of the musician has never been defined better or more succinctly. Whether on stage or in the studio, if you maintain that simple uncluttered thought, you'll do OK.

If you work diligently to achieve your goal—whether you achieve it easily or through a great deal of very hard work, *as most of us do*—others will want to work with you again. The bonus is that what's said about you on the grapevine will be good stuff too. In the Biz it's said that you can't have too many friends, and one enemy is probably too many. Having someone in the recording end of things who respects you and enjoys working with you can only prove helpful.

BREAKS

Tracking can be grueling at times, and you may discover that four hours in the studio is an *e t e r n i t y*. Therefore portions of every session will be given over to breaks. Breaks are important. At times they can be as important as the tracking itself, especially if you're working in a band situation. The rule is, whenever anyone begins to whimper or bleed from the eyeballs, or attempts to strangle the drummer or starts speaking in tongues, it's time for a break.

Breaks are especially important during the mix. If you're going to be involved in the mix, do not attempt to mix too many songs in one session. Professionals work on one song at a time, with no expectation of when it might be complete. If you plan to do more than one tune in any given mix session, you're setting yourself up for frustration. Assume that every song will take forever and surrender when you become fatigued. If you're tired and simply not hearing things right, there's no sense in continuing. Take a break, get away from it, so that later you can hear it fresh again.

THE PERFECT TAKE

If you do a perfect take, that doesn't mean you have *captured* a perfect take. The problems that can screw up a take are myriad, so the time to beam over what you've done is after playback.

A perfect take is not always requisite anyway. Depending on a part's prominence in the final mix, "adequate" may be more than enough. Remember that some sounds will be masked by others, some will become parts of harmonies, and some are orchestrated to go underneath while others surface. Remember, too, that some screw-ups sound good. In fact, in pop music many of the things all the kids take to and walk around imitating are screw-ups. In the studio a vocalist's heart sinks when her voice breaks on a note, but later that shattered note gets her a Grammy. The producer has this understanding in mind when deciding what's acceptable. If he or she says, "Everything sounds good," the point is not to deceive you. In fact, it's to the producer's personal benefit to tell you the truth.

Musicians talk about the *energy,* the *spirit,* the *power,* the *feeling* behind a first take. Typically, however, the perfect take comes only after working through your anxieties. First takes may have the heart, but commonly also have problems. Problems on both sides of the glass are normal during first takes. So be prepared; even if *you* get it right, they may still be working on getting it right in the booth. On subsequent takes usually the mechanics of the performance grow sharper with each take, while the spirit, the heart, the feeling decrease.

When I asked Robben Ford how many takes he needs to nail a solo, he said, "One is desirable, but I *hope* to get it within three takes. Usually, the first one has the best spirit. And, if everybody plays it right—as long as you've got it together technically—the spirit is always best on the first take" (*Bay Blues,* August 1988). But the perfect first take is such an extreme rarity that it might as well be myth.

Running through the progressions, the rhythm, the fingering, and the attack several times seems to be necessary preparation for presenting a tune with an acceptable balance of technical competence and feeling. Once you've gotten the mechanics down, the problem may be to reinstate the spirit. Sometimes it's difficult; sometimes it's impossible. That's why first takes are usually saved, even if they are, admittedly, imperfect. Your first take may be the closest you ever get to capturing that elusive combination of technique and spirit.

After they've nailed a piece, experienced recording artists generally do a couple of extra takes. Once you're in that groove—relaxed, playing well, responding to the music—get a few more shots on tape. Then, after you are sure you've got all that you may need in the can, you might want to try doing a version with a different tempo or a slightly different arrangement before moving on to the next tune.

It's not unusual to spend hours struggling with a routine piece and then, after finally getting it, to kick back and lay out an improvised version that is full of life and superior in every way to the version you struggled over. That doesn't mean that all the work trying to nail the routine piece was wasted. What it means is that all that work was necessary to get you into a position where you could play it a little better. It got your chops up. After you've worked your way through all the pressures and problems and you've successfully captured the piece on tape, take advantage of that position. With the pressure off, while you're relaxed and really rolling, get as much work done as you can. While there's still a clearing in the clouds, bask in the sun. Move on to the next tune and try to nail that elusive perfect take.

SOME RULES WHILE TRACKING

In general, play through your mistakes. Many mistakes can be corrected. Other parts of the tune may prove useful during editing. Even mistakes that can't be corrected can be learned from. Some mistakes are so unique as to actually add to the tune. Occasionally inspiration emerges in the form of a mistake.

Don't vocalize your feelings while tracking. *Think* whatever you want, but keep it inside. The classic situation is this: You've been hammering away on this tune for an hour. Now, suddenly, for the first time, it's working. You're clipping along nicely. It's going great. It's flawless! It's beautiful! You're approaching the end. Prayers go out to whatever god or gods may oversee such things, "Please oh please oh please oh please don't let me screw up now." With three bars to go, a monstrous, glaring, unforgivable, undeniable flub occurs. Your instincts override your wisdom and you mutter something out loud, something you wouldn't say in front of your grandmother.

Then, in playback, the unforgivable mistake that drove you to profanity can't be found. It's just not there. Or it doesn't sound so bad after all. Everything else is just as wonderful, just as solid, just as pure as you thought it was while playing. *The only thing wrong with that take* is your expletive. If only you'd kept your big mouth shut, you would have had a great take. Now you have a legitimate reason to cuss. Which leads directly to . . .

Always keep your vocal mic separate and "off" when not in use. If you've just completed a vocal and the next take is instrumental, you might check it. "Is this mic on? I'd like it off."

If everybody agrees that a take is acceptable, move on. At every point you could probably do better. But, the real question is, is it necessary?

Play every take of each tune *routine* until you nail it.

Focus on *tempo*. It is, perhaps, the most basic characteristic of sound. The reason we cling to a dying note until we're absolutely convinced we can hear it no longer is because we're anticipating that it will repeat. Something deep in our biological construct has us listening, waiting for it to be struck again and begin to establish tempo. That's how basic tempo is. So, while tracking, it's better to hit the wrong note and keep good time than to hit the perfect note out of time. As long as your takes all have a consistent tempo, editing is easy. The most glaring mistake can be remedied by punching in if the tempo is routine.

Don't do anything to any piece of electronic equipment without first asking the engineer or at least—out of courtesy—reporting what you're about to do. Do not adjust any settings on your instrument or other equipment. Do not plug in or unplug. Do not turn anything on or off.

Don't handle microphones. Do not thump them to see if they're on. Do not whistle into an open mic to get the engineer's attention.

After the engineer says, "Rolling," take your time. Slip into it at your own speed. There's no need to rush yourself. If you need to sit for a moment in order to prepare, that's fine. This is not a race.

If you make a false start and can continue playing, continue playing. A false start doesn't mean you have to stop the take. But if you feel you must quit, that's OK also.

Don't worry about whether your reaction to what's going on is normal. There is almost nothing you can do in the studio that hasn't been done before.

Play clean. Effects can be added in the mix. Remember, once the signal has been run through any outboard equipment and recorded, it cannot be *un*-processed. If you need the processed sound, ask for it in your cans.

Anything you do to process the signal makes editing more difficult. If you track clean, you'll be able to edit more easily. When effects are added later, they'll help to obscure the edit. If you track using outboard equipment, when it comes to editing, those same effects will prevent you from editing smoothly. Factors like attack, release, and decay all become a problem in editing. Matching the rate at which reverb diminishes, for example, can be almost impossible. Tracking with effects can set you up for serious problems later.

Of course, if a particular tune is meant to be played in overdrive and you have no reason to believe you'll want to alter it, then go ahead and run it through overdrive. In the studio they can give you the best effects you've ever heard. Another solution, however, is to split the signal. Record effects on a separate track while tracking clean. If the processed track works, use it. If it doesn't, you have the clean track to fall back on.

If you're using any equipment that utilizes batteries—microphones or anything else—be aware that as the batteries deplete, they create distortion and screw up the levels.

Going directly into the board can be very difficult if you're not used to it. There's no amp sound, no ambiance. If someone suggests a *direct box,* be aware of the difficulties that may arise.

If you're planning to mic your amp, it had better be a good amp and set up for the studio. Microphones cannot improve the sound of poor equipment. Lousy sound picked up by the best microphone available and recorded on the best tape machine available is only lousy sound nicely captured.

Don't expect playback on every take. Playback is disruptive. It takes a lot of time. Usually the engineer, when satisfied that there is enough tape, will initiate playback. If you ask for playback, though, you won't be denied. But if you're going to take the time for playback, be sure also to take the time to listen carefully and critically.

Stay put in the studio. One of the biggest wastes of time for first-timers (and others who should know better) is going into the booth to listen to every playback. Professionals do it because the monitors in the booth offer superior sound. But that doesn't mean it's the right thing to do. Engineers usually put up with it rather than open up the debate as to who's the boss, but it's a huge waste of everybody's time. Artists who know what they're doing simply sit or take the opportunity to stand up and stretch or walk around in the studio during playback.

Playback does sound different through the headphones than through the monitors. It also sounds different on different monitors. And many times, for the artist, there seems to be almost no relationship to how the music sounded in the studio.

Before going into the session, decide on a set number of attempts you'll make before moving on. If you simply cannot nail a tune in that number of shots, move on. At that point, ask the engineer if there is enough to work with. Ask for the producer's opinion. Maybe they'll encourage you to take one final shot. Otherwise, move on to the next tune. If it just ain't workin', admit it. Come back to it again later, when you feel more comfortable.

Don't scrap a take because it's merely "acceptable." Acceptable takes can prove invaluable in the mix. Depending upon how much time you have left, the acceptable take may be the best thing you've got. Later, in sequencing, the solid comfort of an acceptable cut may work nicely as an interlude between more finely orchestrated tunes.

After the last note has been struck and died down, wait at least to the count of three before speaking. During that time do not move or set the instrument down or make any noise of any sort. It's a good idea, in fact, to let the engineer be the first to speak at the end of a take. If the take seems perfect, let silence be the perfect herald of your joy.

Bring snacks and something to drink. The process is draining enough without low blood sugar. Keep that stuff out of the studio proper, though. And out of the booth.

Don't eat late in the session. You may think, "Hey, if we go get something to eat, I'll perk right up," but eating actually slows you down. It's a biological fact. If you run out and get a late-night meal, you might as well just wrap it up.

GOING OFF SCHEDULE

The idea of playing music sometimes gets lost in the struggle to capture sound. And when things aren't going right, tracking can become an excruciating process. If it starts to become unbearable and looks like it soon might become impossible, you're better going off schedule and doing something unplanned than continuing to pound your head against the studio wall. Going off schedule is a tough call, though, because it *will* set things back. On the other hand, it may also save the project.

If you go off schedule, make it a time of fun. Set aside whatever you've been working on, forget about all that for a while, and simply play. Work on your back-up tunes. This takes the pressure off but doesn't allow you to drift too far.

Here's some advice. Instruct your producer that anytime you go off schedule, the engineer should roll tape. Simply roll tape. It's a rare opportunity in the studio to improvise, and some great stuff can occur while you're frustrated and playing from the gut. I remember seeing Lonnie Brooks play a blistering set (at Larry Blake's in Berkeley) one night. During the break I overheard the bass player say, "Man, I sure wish we could get her to piss him off every night!"

Here's Charlie Musselwhite on the subject of unscheduled inspiration:

Sometimes a tune will just sort of show up by itself—that's how I can best describe it. These things will just occur. It's like a spirit comes into the room and everybody just falls into this groove. Nobody came to the session with that in mind. You can't predict it at all. It'll just click all of a sudden. It might be early in the session, or it might be late at night, like a second wind or something. You might be exhausted, but all of a sudden you feel rejuvenated and this thang just hits *everybody*. You're playing and . . . "Hey, where did this come from?" You're looking at everybody and laughing, like "We don't know what it is, but we're on it and it's takin' us." *Those are the times you're hopin' the guy in the control room has the tape going.* You can't stop and say, "Let's start over again" because you'll lose it.

Whatever the results of this little diversion, go back on schedule as soon as you can. The idea that you can simply continue to improvise for the remainder of the project is tempting nonsense, but it's nonsense nonetheless.

ROUGH-MIX TAPES

During the session it is difficult to retain objectivity. So at the end of each session, you'll be given a rough mix of the session. That tape will help to put things in perspective. It'll let you know where you stand in the project, so that you can correct your problems and move on in the next session. The tape is a reference. When you listen to it, you'll be able to see what's good and should remain, what you have yet to do, and what you need to do over.

Bear in mind that it is a *rough* mix. It may be recorded at levels that sound all wrong. But if the engineer offers to spend some time and give you an especially fine rough mix, do not accept the offer. The intention may be good, but it's a waste of time. If you listen at lower volumes, you'll be less distracted. Bear in mind that at home you'll be playing it back on different equipment anyway, over lesser speakers, at different volumes than it was recorded at, in a room that's not designed for focused, critical listening.

If the engineer has not labeled the tape or has labeled it insufficiently, label the tape. Do that before leaving the studio. Tapes easily get lost. Make a habit of labeling them correctly. The label should include your name and phone number, the name of the project, the session number, and the date. List the artists involved. Put anything on the label that will help you to know, six months down the road, what's on the tape without having to play it. If there is an especially tasty cut that you want to save, be sure to note that on the label. Devise a symbol that indicates there's something especially valuable on a tape. Otherwise, sometime in the future, after listening to the first few seconds, you may toss it or be tempted to tape over it. Do not label the J card; label the tape mechanism itself.

While listening to the rough mix, take notes. You'll want to ask the engineer any questions you may have about the mix, of course, but what you really want from this tape is to determine *how you are doing.* Concentrate on your own work: things like musicianship, the presentation of the tune itself.

Readjust your schedule after listening to the tape if that appears necessary. If you're ahead of schedule or if you're behind schedule, your producer needs to get on the phone and let the studio know about any changes. They'll be setting up for your arrival, and if you've changed your schedule but haven't informed the studio, they may not be too happy about it. They'll have to set up again, on your time. While they do, you'll be standing around waiting. That's a terrible way to start any session. Sessions that start out badly are almost certain to escalate into something worse.

If you have a few days between sessions and the rough mix reveals some problems, remember that worrying over mistakes between sessions isn't going to help. In fact, working on mistakes between sessions may, in certain ways, only complicate matters. For example, if you work out a remedy to a problem at home, then go back into the studio and can't duplicate your solution, how is that going to make you feel? Do not waste time at home going over problems that can only be fixed in the studio. If you're good enough to be in the studio at all, you're good enough to correct your problems, or at least try to, during the next session. Rely on your skills.

The exception, of course, is if you're recording digitally and have all the right equipment at home to make those corrections in a professional manner. If you can do your corrections at home and then fly them in at the studio, by all means do so. But make sure you're recording at the same sampling rate.

If there's only good news on the rough-mix tape, be sure to listen to it again just before returning to the studio. That will give you the lift you need to dive back into the work with renewed enthusiasm. So play it on the way to the studio.

Hey, you know, this sounds pretty dang good!

Save all rough-mix tapes until the conclusion of the project. If there is anything good on one, save it. A highly respected producer with years in the business admits, "Many is the time I've mixed something, then listened to the two-track from the session and realized I had mixed the life out of it." If that happens, the tape from the previous session will help the engineer to re-establish things more quickly to their former glory.

PROBLEMS DUE TO CONVERSION

Because the frequency range and the dynamic range of digital are both much greater than those of analog, any time you go from analog to digital (A/D) or digital to analog (D/A), you may be surprised, if not disappointed, in the results.

D/A If at any point in the process, you go from digital to analog tape, the limitations of the tape itself become a factor. If, for example, you plan to go to cassettes from the digital mix, there can be problems. When you hear what's on DAT played back on analog, a lot of sound may literally be missing. Analog tape is incapable of carrying the extreme high and low ends that digital handles. Subtler, quiet passages—which come across nicely in digital—may be buried in noise (produced by both tape and machinery) that simply isn't present in the digital format. And low-end stuff will necessarily be cut off or distorted.

If your final product will be cassettes, and your mix is going to be digitally mastered, be sure to make analog tapes during the mix. And be sure to listen to those tapes for the differences described above. What you hear on digital is *not* representative of what the final analog tape will sound like.

A/D If you capture anything on analog and go to digital for the mix, it will all be there. But in digital the bass and overall amplitude are dispersed over such a wide dynamic range that things usually play back quieter and thinner. Another way to look at that is, analog plays back both louder and fatter than digital. When you go to digital, it may sound unacceptably thin.

This stuff can be, and should be, adjusted in the mix, but you should be aware of it. And, if your final product is going to both CD and cassette, you will need two masters, each produced with different considerations.

MULTITRACKING FOR BANDS

Here's one of the ways a successful band might do it. They come in as a herd, do a rough mix of the rhythm section. Go home, work out the details about how they're going to do the vocals. They come back in, cut a reference vocal. With the reference vocal in place, they start serious work on the basic rhythm tracks. They start out with the drummer playing solo with the rough mix or a click track. The drummer works until they're satisfied that they have enough good takes. From this point, everyone builds on what the drummer has done. Next comes the bass, then rhythm guitar.

Between each session they take home a rough mix to decide how much more work each track might need. They come back in to finalize the basic tracks, over-dubbing to fatten things up where needed, and doing basic orchestration. They go home with a rough mix of the basic tracks and the scratch vocal on top.

Each instrumental solo is then added one at a time. Then the vocals are cut in the following session or two. After the vocals are in place, there are sessions for adding sweetener. At that point every track and every take are looked at critically. Solos may be done over, overdubbed, and tweaked. Then they begin the mix, which takes typically, oh, say, roughly ten to twelve thousand years.

Take what information you can from that. Your project will necessarily be a somewhat streamlined version. On your project schedule, for your first session (basic tracks or bedtracks) you'll need drums, bass, rhythm guitar, and vocalist. After a run-through, a reasonable attempt at nailing any basic track is maybe a dozen takes. If you just can't make it work in that amount of time, switch gears, try one of the other tunes. Maybe going back to the first tune after you feel more comfortable will help.

Once you've got a satisfactory take on the first tune, let the engineer know you're ready to attempt the next one. The basic tracks for two tunes will reasonably fill up one session and likely carry over to a second session. If you get two of the three rhythm tracks down in one session, you're doing excellent work. If things are going exceptionally well, you'll record the rhythm tracks for several tunes in the same session. Whatever your pace, though, a good producer may help you to bring that time down considerably.

Drummers are used to starting things out, so tracking the drum solo can go pretty easily. On the other hand, good drummers also make continual reference to the other players. So if there's a problem tracking the drummer solo, record the rhythm section ensemble. It's quicker and easier all around.

Otherwise, once you get the drums for all three tunes, send the drummer away, with the instruction to check in by phone in a couple of hours. Then work with the bass for those tunes. Once you get that track, send the bass player away. The excitement can disappear pretty quickly if people just sit around waiting for their turn again, and nobody wants somebody pacing around, getting underfoot. It's better to send players away and ask that they check in later, at a specified time.

Be careful not to get so involved in laying down basic tracks that you run out of studio time. Typically, vocals and instrumentals take at least as much time as basic tracks. Plan for that and stick with the project schedule. If you find yourself still tinkering with basic tracks in the third session, in terms of this first project, something is wrong; do what you can to finish up. Maybe it's time to book additional sessions or decide that, this time in, you're going to concentrate on getting just one good tune recorded.

If you get things done faster than scheduled, congratulations. You now have to decide whether you want to try to get started on your backup tunes while you've still got time slated. Before you leave the studio after your session, take the time to go over the schedule with the studio personnel. "OK, next session, we're gonna be tracking the horn section."

AN EXEMPLARY TALE

In September of 1988, I was invited into the studio to watch a blues band record a little original blues. The single came out in December of that year. If you look on the label, one tune plays for 2 minutes 55 seconds, the flip side for about the same time. It took somewhat longer to record, however, something in the vicinity of a week. Although each of the musicians involved had recorded before, it was their first time in the studio as a unit.

They'd already been at it a couple of days when I arrived one night at around 2 A.M., and things were not going well. This particular session had gotten underway in the evening, and by the time I came in the door, civility had gone out the window. Everyone was either irritable or smoldering or loopy. The producer, who'd made a name for himself professionally by working with the Tubes, was hunkered over the console in sullen silence. When he spoke at all, it was in an ominous whisper. In his voice I thought I detected, not just exasperation, but regret for having undertaken the project.

The band was struggling valiantly to maintain composure while the guitar player attempted to punch in a bridge between vocals. It was just a little riff, something he'd played literally a thousand times before, on stage. But he didn't like the results he was getting on tape. Although the other members of the band assured him that it sounded good, he insisted on doing it again. And again and again. Each time they rolled back the tape and listened intently to the playback. The producer made occasional diplomatic attempts to nudge the guitar player onward but couldn't convince him.

In theory the guitar player should have gotten points for diligence. In reality he was driving everybody crazy. They were all acutely aware of the fact that they were running out of studio time. It got to the point where no matter what he did, as soon as he finished, everybody jumped to their feet and vociferously proclaimed it to be great. Yes, sir, a stellar moment in guitar-playing history. But there was a hollowness in their praise, as if they were trying to convince themselves.

One of the most serious decisions first-timers face is knowing when to quit. It may be nobler in the mind to take up arms against a sea of troubles (and, by opposing, end them), but what's noble and what's prudent are often different matters. In short, there is a point at which you should quit. There is a point at which you should say, "We just can't get any work done here today."

If you can't get it right in a certain amount of time, then maybe it's not going to happen. You're not going to get it right in 20 hours if you didn't get it right in 5.

A more serious dilemma is knowing that you probably should quit . . . but can't Being forced to continue tracking simply because you're running out of studio time is not conducive to getting the best stuff on tape. This is what was happening with this blues band.

While the struggle in the studio continued, some girls who'd been hanging around, waiting for the party to begin, made a pretty good decision. They got up and left without ceremony. I took their departure as an indication that it was time for me to move on too. Although everyone seemed to be in reasonable restraint at the moment, the party was definitely over and I wanted to escape before the serious backbiting got underway. In a situation like this, someone has to take the blame, and the most common scenario has everybody pointing anywhere but in the mirror.

Of course, it was a mystery to these guys how things had gotten so far out of hand. They thought they'd done everything right. They'd consolidated their repertoire; they were in there to record only two tunes. They had a big-time producer. They'd booked a good studio with state-of-the-art equipment. Unfortunately, they'd done a lot wrong also. Neither song was routine. The producer was also acting engineer. Worse yet, he was a friend of the struggling guitar player, so his authority was somewhat fettered. And the band's budget didn't allow for enough time in the studio to complete the project. Mystery solved.

That session lasted long after I'd left, but I can't imagine how. Nevertheless, the single, when it came out, held a couple of solid cuts of meat 'n' potatoes blues. Good stuff. Few listeners would ever guess what a struggle it had been. When I listened to it, I was unable to determine which part it was that had given them so much trouble.

The message is, however much fun recording may appear to be from the outside, it is a demanding, at times arduous process. It's easy to get side-tracked, waylaid, and inextricably entangled in the process. In fact, the better the work you're doing, the more focused you are, the more serious and dedicated to the task, the easier it is for these things to occur. Strangely, the more intent you are on your goal, the easier it is to get lost.

But the same coping skills that get a person through life can get them through a recording session—planning, organization, common sense, courtesy, luck, knowing when to take a break or quit, and the occasional, seemingly random outburst of lunatic absurdity.

Recording is a complicated, heady, draining process during which time and reason become distorted.

AN INTERVIEW

Lowell Fulson's recording career spans more than 50 years. Think about that for one second. Fifty years. With the rare exceptions of John Lee Hooker, Gatemouth Brown, and Rufus Thomas, there is no one in the music business today who has that kind of continuous studio experience. Fulson first went into a recording studio in 1946, with blues entrepreneur Bob Geddins at the board. They recorded a blues tune called "Three O'clock in the Morning," which Fulson had written and Geddins had arranged. It later became B.B. King's first hit, one of many Lowell Fulson songs King has gotten good use out of.

In the early 1950s Fulson teamed up with pianist/arranger Lloyd Glenn, who turned out to be the perfect catalyst for bringing out Fulson's genius. After meeting Glenn, Lowell Fulson quickly developed a full range of styles, from the simplest down-home guitar blues to the most sophisticated stylings backed by orchestral arrangements.

Lowell Fulson is a remarkable talent. As a guitarist, vocalist, and songwriter, he has influenced some of the music's greatest artists. His unique, cool, uncluttered approach to guitar work has played a decisive role in the development of artists like Pee Wee Crayton and Robben Ford. His deeply personal, yet always gentlemanly approach to vocals intrigued a young Bobby "Blue" Bland so much that he admits to having imitated Fulson's phrasing for years before finding his own voice. Fulson's rendition of "Everyday I Have the Blues" is a blues standard. And Charlie Musselwhite tells me, "Magic Sam got his style from him too, you know." Magic Sam cited Lowell Fulson as his "first major influence." As a songwriter, Fulson has had a tremendous output. He has penned dozens of unforgettable tunes, among them "Reconsider Baby" and "Black Nights"—just two of Fulson's masterpieces.

His most recent recording session took place for Bull's Eye in 1996. But by 1954 he'd attracted enough attention to inspire the Chess brothers to sign him. In the interim, he has also recorded with Arhoolie, Blue Rock'it, Rounder, and a dozen smaller independent labels. In short, Lowell Fulson has been around and he knows some stuff.

You'll want to note that, while talking about recording, Fulson mentions budget, scheduling, preproduction, routining, the producer, the skills of the musicians he's worked with, and editing and mixing. He states directly how much hard work recording usually is, even for someone with as many years as he's had in the studio. He also talks about the importance of taking breaks, going off schedule, and matters that are important to consider before going in. The interview from which these excerpts are taken was recorded on February 18, 1997. It has been edited for continuity.

I was nervous going into the interview because I'd interviewed Lowell Fulson before and knew him to be an unassuming, solitary man. It's difficult to get him to open up, and there's something even a little unfair about trying. On top of that, I'm sometimes reduced to a stammering idiot when faced with talking to people whose work I admire, and I have admired Lowell Fulson's work for years. I've never missed an opportunity to stand right at the apron of the stage, grinning like an idiot, while his music rained down on me. So the ringing sound of Tina Mayfield answering the phone was a welcome relief. "Don't hang up now, baby; let me clear the line. . . . Don't hang up now, sweetie, I'll go get Lowell."

RF: Mr. Fulson, I'd like to talk to you a bit about recording . . .
LF: I don't know what to tell you. What are you lookin' for?

RF: Well, do you have any tales you can tell us, you know, something about how much *fun* recording can be?
LF: No, I wish it was, though. It's mostly hard work in the studio. It's a lot of hard work in the studio. But if you're pleased, it makes it lots easier. If you're pleased with what they're doin', you'll be all right.

RF: You're talking about the producer?
LF: Yeah. And the arranger. Sometimes they do the arrangement too. Keep your eye on the guy who's puttin' out the thang. Sometimes they're good and sometimes they're not so good.

RF: You've managed to work with some good ones, though. Bob Geddins, whom you worked with in the forties, did arrangements for you, and together you put out a few hits. What was the name of that first tune back in '46?
LF: "Three O'clock in the Morning." I followed it with "Western Union Man," I think.

RF: How much has recording changed since 1946? Is it much easier these days?
LF: Well, they're two different products. Back then, if you wanted to electrify it . . . well, you'd have to spend the time . . . you'd want to go for music that didn't have a whole lot of horns to it. You know, that's why you'd electrify it.

RF: And Lloyd Glenn . . . I know he did arrangements for you.
LF: Yeah, Lloyd, well, he was m'boy. Yeah, we'd get together, you know, do some talkin' to each other. And the songs that gave us the most trouble in rehearsal, we'd first try to knock out all the kinks involved, and then go in and cut the record then.

RF: You're suggesting resolving this stuff *before* going into the studio?
LF: Yeah.

RF: After you felt like you had all the kinks knocked out, then you'd go in?
LF: Yeah. That's what I meant.

RF: Is there any advice you might want to pass on to kids going into the studio for the first time?
LF: I would tell them this: Be sure you know what you're gonna do, and that you want to do it, before you attempt to do it. And that'll give you the will power to go on when it gets to goin' a little rough, you know.

RF: . . . and when the going gets rough?
LF: Just go out and sit out and cool off. Your arranger should usually know when you need lettin' alone. So they'll see you sharin' a conversation [arguing], whatever, with some man and he'll say, "They don't know, man. It'll be OK."

RF: So an important part of the producer's job is to give you a break when you need it, huh?

LF: Yeah, give you a break. Or leave you alone if you're that kind of artist. Some artists don't want to be left alone, you know, and some guys do. He can do his part better if he'd said, "You want to be by yourself?" That's what it takes for you to cut it sometimes.

RF: How much preproduction do you do?

LF: It kinda depends quite a bit on the size group you're workin' with. When I was with Bob, there wasn't nothin' but a couple of us: me and my brother [Martin Fulson played second guitar on the earliest sessions]. Later we got a trio and now it's a combo. But it's something that, you know, you're gonna have to study. A big band, or even a medium-sized band, sometimes will give you a little difficulty if you don't have the men. . . . You know, some of that stuff you write down, you can't put it on charts. And we'd get into somethin'. "That's not like you said on the sheet." Or "Well, come on man, let's make it into something like this here, then." And you don't press it, you know?

Sometimes an artist can be sittin' around playin' for you, and find them little old notes where ordinarily you wouldn't think about foolin' with 'em, 'cause you'd just be goin' on followin' with a pattern. But sometimes you see where it's gonna cause you a little trouble, and you just throw out a hand, "Anybody got *any* ideas? Got any ideas?" You have to try to feel your way through . . . and you just hope, a lot of the time, you hope your man will—an artist will—pull you out, you know? If he's got a pretty good talent, he can pull you out when you think you're really in a bind.

RF: So in the studio do you always play each tune at the same tempo?

LF: Well, they've got machines now can slow it down to just about what you want. But back in them days, they didn't have all of that, you know. So you'd try to get close to it. In these times, they take it from one state—he lives here, you live over there—and that's how it comes to the timin' that you're talkin' about . . . blend the first part in with the second part. But they got these machines now, can slow that tape down just a hair. They do a lot of things they couldn't do back then.

RF: So in those days you set up live as a complete unit. Do you still continue to record live as a unit?

LF: Yeah. A lot of times they'll take the whole band and set 'em down and keep just the rhythm and go back and cut the tracks. It depends on how many pieces and how bad you're tryin' to say somethin'.

RF: So, I guess in earlier times you didn't do overdubbing the same as you might do it these days?

LF: Well, we called it *piece it up a little bit.* Yeah, it was about the same. It's just if there was more of it to tape, it would take more to finish the product than it would now. I mean, back then you couldn't hardly, you couldn't dub in. . . . I mean you could but, God, it would take like a separate day just to do that.

RF: And how much did you have to say about editing?

LF: Long time ago I played by myself with the guitar, sang the song, and Bob would dub it. That's when the dubbin' would come in, you know. We'd call it piecin' it up . . . take out one word and put in another word. "This part of the sentence is all right, but further down there it's not as good." And he'd take that out. But we wouldn't be there a lot of the time. We'd just take a week off.

RF: So, in those days, you didn't have any hand in the mix? You just left it up to the producer?

LF: Yeah, well, you would tell him. And he didn't have too much to remember in the first place. It depends on how they hooked up with you.

RF: Today do you sit in on the mix?

LF: Well, you can if you want to, because they can cut in all around you, and *you* got one thing and *he* can be cuttin' around you, savin' that for somethin' else, you know. You mostly leave it up to your arranger, your producer, because naturally you'd tell him what you wanted and everything. And after you leave the studio, they go through and see, "Would that sound better, or fit any better than this would?" And then, after you've gone—ain't there to be criticizin' while the man's workin'—he'll go on when you're not around to put his work down. And another thing is, it depends upon the budget they've got. They cut the session short, cut the album short, and then they have to go and get some more money before you get through.

RF: The budget's important?

LF: Sometimes they wouldn't have enough time. A lot of artists need a little more time on something, you know what I mean? And they don't have enough. A lot of artists hurry to finish a product up when it's not quite ready yet. And I've heard them say afterwards, they'd say, "Man! I coulda done better than that!"

RF: But these days the producers who come to you usually have the bucks to see a project through. They've come to you because they like your work and they want to work with you.

LF: Well, just about. Sometimes you get lucky with somethin'.

RF: Do you feel like the publishing industry has treated you fairly? Do you feel like you're getting royalties on everything . . . all that's coming to you from the publishing industry?

LF: Well, not everything. But it wouldn't do me no good to go on about it, because, you know, they have their excuses [shared laughter]. You just smile and go ahead on.

8

· ·
THE MIX
· ·

MIXING AND TRACKING are different processes with different considerations and each demanding an entirely different focus. Most studio professionals recommend keeping the tasks separated by at least a day because the mix-down requires fresh ears and the utmost attention. Quite naturally, however, everyone at this point is pretty eager to get their hands on a finished product. So the first question asked, predictably enough, is, how long is it going to take? The answer is, if you stay out of the way, it will take a lot less time than if you feel you need to be in on it.

The mix is crucial to the outcome of all your work in the studio. Therefore many artists balk at the idea of abandoning their work at such a critical point. They feel that too much is at stake to simply turn the task over to the engineer. Others choose to have nothing to do with the mix. They stay out of the process altogether, with the exception of final approval. In general, the consensus of studio professionals seems to be that artists *should* stay entirely out of the mix—*if* they've got a good producer. Obviously, if you don't have someone you're sure of to represent you, you'll need to stay with the engineer. After all, that person will be making technical decisions that will permanently affect the aesthetics of your music.

The results of the mix are unquestionably your concern. It's both natural and right that you'll want to be there. You'll want to be sure that quality is not lost and that anything that is not quite right remains out. In the mix the artist's intentions must be clearly defined and jealously defended. Miles Davis said, "It takes years of playing, just to play like yourself." Such hard-won accomplishment is justifiably protected. But the artist needs to bear in mind that the engineer shares the desire to get a good mix and is invested in the outcome too.

It's difficult to participate in any process that you don't understand entirely. Yet that is precisely what musicians do when they demand their right to participate in the mix. They interfere in matters that should probably be left in the hands of others with more experience. As in every phase of the recording process, the best advice for first-timers is to bow to the expertise of the paid professionals. In the mix they'll be considering matters that you may not even be aware of. Depend on them.

Bands have their own problems. The main problem is that everyone wants to be involved. No one wants to be left out. That means everybody in the booth, all interjecting and all ignoring the fact that any change in any track affects the entire tape. The bass player wants the bass up louder, the guitarist wants the guitar up louder, the drummer wants the drums up, and then the singer doesn't feel like the vocal is on top anymore. If the engineer gives everyone everything they want, the result is cacophony. And, of course, it can be pretty difficult to make adjustments to Lou's solo if Lou is standing right behind you watching your every move. For the sake of the project, you want only one person there. Everybody else, go home.

If you can remain quiet, you might want to sit in just for the experience. It will make you appreciate all the work your engineer is doing for you. It will give you some real insight into why some things were done the way they were during tracking. That's one process that sometimes makes a little more sense in hindsight. So it won't hurt to go in and observe, and it may actually help you with future projects. If nothing else, it will probably eliminate any further desire to sit in on future mix-down sessions. After a couple of hours spent with a really good, really meticulous mix engineer, even the most protective artist will usually be looking around anxiously for any excuse to get out of that room.

Mixing is an arduous process. It's the slowest-moving and the most tedious part of the recording process that the artist might choose to have a hand in. A large part of it is not just making adjustments but trying them out to see how they sound before they are committed to tape. "Let's see how this sounds" can go on forever.

One producer warns: "One of the hardest things in the studio is to keep your listening disciplined while keeping your ears fresh too. You do not want to be so sick of the tune by the time you're done mixing that you're willing to accept anything, just to be done with it. I mean, after you've heard it thirty or forty times in a row, there's a part of you that doesn't even want to hear it anymore." In fact, there's a point at which you're so familiar with the thing that mistakes may actually begin to sound OK. It's not that they are, in fact, OK; it's only that you've heard them so many times that your mind begins to accommodate them. Such mistakes will stick out like a sore thumb the following day if you're lucky. If you're not so lucky, they'll show up again only after pressing.

If you have no desire to get involved, the first couple of hours of mixing is a good time for you to go somewhere else and unwind. This is the point at which you've earned a beer or two. Stick your nose in after an hour to see how things are going—the engineer may have questions—but step aside and let others do what you've hired them to do. It's in their hands. It's out of yours.

Not only is it acceptable to stay out of the mix entirely, but it's also reasonable. If you stay out, you'll be able to fairly evaluate what you hear when you finally do get a chance to listen to what's transpired. So in a very real sense, staying out of the mix can be an important part of your task. Many professional recording artists have no hand in the mix by choice. Others have no choice whatsoever.

Charlie Musselwhite:

> Here [in the mix] is where I have a problem. It's a fairly common problem with musicians. There are certain tones in my hearing that are gone now. Well, here's an example: I spent a lot of time mixing this one particular project, and at the end of the day, I would take the tape and play it for other people. On this particular tape the cymbals were way up on top, just crashing away, and people kept saying, "Well, it all sounds pretty good, but what's with those cymbals?" And I asked, "What cymbals?" I didn't hear the cymbals at all. For me they didn't exist. To other people they were really loud and really distracting and *way* up on top. I don't know how it got mixed like that. Maybe the engineer just thought I liked cymbals. But I don't hear birds singing, I don't hear telephones when they ring sometimes. The sound just isn't there. So for mixing, I'm really a cripple. I like to help out on it a little, but I know the final say shouldn't be mine.

Here's something the pros know that you may not: every nicely recorded track does not have to become part of your mix. If something sounds good *and it enhances the music,* use it. If it doesn't, take it out. If you're having difficulty with a track, the answer to making it work may not be as simple as adjusting the levels; it may be simpler still—scrap that track altogether. Every skilled artist in every field recognizes the value of white space. Just because the track is dynamic, wonderful, even perfect, does not necessarily mean that it improves the mix. Here's where good producers can prove very helpful, since their job is to decide how an artist's objectives for a project might best be accomplished. Not being personally involved, the producer can be dispassionate about which part needs to be cut when there's just too much going on.

Scrapping a track does not mean that all your work on it is lost or wasted. That track may serve as the backbone of a later tune, so set it aside. Most artists have wonderful scrap ends (outtakes) sitting around waiting for use in some later masterpiece. If you have something really wonderful but it's getting in the way, save it to DAT. Tap into its wonder in some future session.

You can feel safe turning your work over to others to be mixed. If at this point the producer and engineer do not know what you're after, it's probably too late. If they do know what you want, they're going to try to achieve that. If the engineer has done a good job and produced a tape that is hot, the mix should go smoothly. After each mix session, they'll send you home with a tape. If you don't like some part of it, one person goes back in to point out the problem. At the end of that session, you'll get another tape.

If you want to discuss it, discuss it at home. Make notes.

THE MIX-DOWN PROCESS

1. Select the best takes from all tracks.

2. Assign each track to a position in the 180-degree sound field.

3. Set EQ on each track.

4. Orchestrate the tune by riding the gain (adjusting the volume) on each track for the duration of the tune.

5. Edit, taking out unwanted blips and replacing screw-ups with acceptable passages from other takes (this is why it's important to have all your songs routined, to establish a tempo for each tune, and to do all the takes at that same tempo).

6. Prepare the tape for mastering.

The mix has to do with establishing an overall EQ, as well as the orchestration of each tune. Simply put, that means deciding which sound should be on top at any given point and which should go underneath. If, while on stage, everybody in the band just charges ahead full tilt, wide open, the result is bedlam. Live audiences sometimes go wild over such madness. On record, however, such stuff is plainly just noise.

Creating good ensemble music on stage is a matter of orchestration. Everybody backs off while the vocalist sings a quiet little phrase. The tempo is cut for the rest of the crew while the drummer goes wild on the tom-toms. The rhythm guitarist and the vocalist step back while the bass player steps to the edge of the stage, featured as a soloist. In recording, the mix is the equivalent of that kind of orchestration. When the violins shoot up over the top, flutter in the clear blue eternity for a bit before plummeting downward in ever-widening spirals, to settle softly underneath the vocals again, that's done in the mix. And though it may not be the part people walk around humming, it's the part that makes that song great. The mix is about turning takes into music. The mix is the place where songs become great.

There are a lot of different approaches to the task. Capturing every channel's unique character is what tracking is about. Ensuring that each track takes its place in the mix without losing its unique character is an important part of what the mix is about.

Some engineers try to get a general balance at first and then go back in and tweak the individual tracks. Others work on each individual track systematically, one at a time, and then see where that's gotten them before making further adjustments. Others approach the mix in the same order in which the tracks were recorded. Build up the rhythm section first—drums, bass, rhythm guitar—then go back and add in secondary elements such as background vocals, calling limiters, compression, and noise reduction into play when required. Add in harmony and work with that. Then add in the lead vocal and finally, sweetener.

It's a process of adjusting levels, playing it through, hammering down anything that sticks out. Playing it through again. Knocking off the rough edges. Playing it through again. Automated mixing consoles recall the moves the engineer makes throughout this process, so that the adjustments become progressively finer. Sometimes the engineer is making decisions about one track, sometimes decisions concerning more than one track. Since adjustments to any track have an effect on the positioning of other tracks in the mix, it's a balancing act. Sometimes the focus is on refining one section of a song or smoothing out the transitions between sections or making decisions about a phrase or even a single note. It's a process of constant roll-back, endless playback, and critical listening.

Whatever the approach, slowly but surely the engineer and the producer together orchestrate the mix by establishing the levels, the spatial placement, the EQ of each track, and tightening the focus. It's a matter of systematically zeroing in on the artist's preconceived idea of what the tune should, or could, sound like until the artist is happy and the work is reduced to two tracks of stereo sound.

For your own purposes, you'll want to review all outtakes and archive tapes before going to the mix. Listen carefully and make a note of anything you want in, as well as anything you want out of, the final mix. When you listen to the final mix, go through and systematically check again to see that these things are either absent (if that's what you want) or present. You'll want to catch these things before your work is sent off to be mastered. You'll also want to make an archival copy of the final mix on DAT. This copy is called a *safety* or an archival master. If your mix is stored digitally, it's pretty safe.*

SEQUENCING

Take the time to give some consideration to the order of the tunes on your tape. The selection and order of the pieces on your master are important. Consider tempo, key signature, mood, and the different instruments that are featured. There should be variety from one cut to the next, but each piece should, at the same time, be representative of your work.

Start off with your best cut. This is no longer the tune you play best; it's the one that grabs the most immediate attention. If you've got one that grabs 'em in the first bar, that's good. One that grabs 'em with the first note is better. If, during tracking, a tune emerges decidedly as the best cut, place it as the first cut, A side. At this point, all the tunes should be wonderful. If they are not, reschedule, go back in, and make them so.

General wisdom dictates to start out, first cut, up tempo, and end with something thoughtful. If you're going to cassette, you'll need that arrangement on both sides. If you have lengthy tunes, drop them in somewhere in the middle. Remember, on CD the entire program must remain approximately under 75 minutes.

* The Audio Engineering Society's recommendation to the industry is that companies back up digital tapes with analog tape safety masters. They've discovered that the tape transport mechanism on DAT tapes can become warped and render the tape unusable after several years of storage (*Billboard*, July 19, 1997).

With cassettes the longer program always goes on the A side. Obviously, that doesn't apply if you're going to CD. Consequently, you have the opportunity to resequence your tunes if you'll be producing both cassettes and CDs. Think about the order of your tunes as another opportunity to be creative.

EDITING AND MIXING

From all indications, editing is a crucial point for both the artist and the engineer. For some reason, studio professionals who have surrendered to your demands throughout the entire project can become stubborn, unyielding, and even demanding when it comes to editing and mixing *your* work. Your task is to get what you want without getting embroiled in endless bickering over minutia or rupturing the business relationship so badly it can never be repaired. I can't tell you how to do that; I can, however, forewarn you that such squabbles are a fairly common occurrence during editing.

One time I found myself struggling for a couple hours, trying to get an engineer to leave a little tail on the end of one of my pieces. It was just two notes struck after the song's completion, an involuntary muscle twitch. I thought those notes wrapped things up nicely, though. For strictly professional reasons, the engineer wanted them out. He was pretty stubborn about it too.

I'd known this guy for a couple of years. He is not only a far better musician than I'll ever be; he also has more knowledge about sound recording stuck between his teeth, after brushing, than I'll ever wring from my entire dog-eared collection of *Mix* back issues. Nevertheless, I took a stance. I wanted those notes in. He wanted them out. We would argue about it for a while, then I'd let it drop. I'd suffer in silence for a bit before bringing it up again.

Each time he calmly explained why the notes shouldn't be in there. And he was right, of course. There's no reason to have two badly struck, orphan notes muddling up an otherwise nice tune. And getting rid of such stuff was, after all, what we were in there for. But each time I calmly explained that he was working for me and no matter how idiotic my request, it should be honored. He begrudgingly put the notes back in and played it back while shaking his head with unnecessarily exaggerated derision. Everything in him rebelled upon hearing those two wayward notes. As we listened, he actually ground his teeth. I listened and liked what I heard. The anarchy in my soul responded nicely to those superfluous notes. Eventually, just so we could get on with things, the notes were cut. But not forgotten. I still think they should be restored.

This is the sort of thing that goes on between engineer and artist in the mix. It demonstrates nicely, once again, the differing points of view that can exist in the studio.

Dale Miller has had similar experiences:

> In the mix—it depends. It's a combination of how much you trust the other
> people and how much you want to get involved. I've always been pretty

involved in that sort of thing. And I'm not afraid to go against recommendations, although with solo guitar there's not too much more involved than EQ-ing the instrument. I personally like vocals lower than most records, and I fight engineers over that all the time. I'm not afraid to say, "Hey, I want it lower, and that's just the way it's gonna be." It depends on the particular artist, how much you want to get involved.

PREPARING YOUR TAPE FOR MASTERING

After mixing, the next step in postproduction is preparing the tape for mastering. If you plan on using more than one format, say, cassette and CD, you'll want to provide two masters, each meeting the individual requirements of one format.

Preparing the tape for mastering means:

• Determining playing times and time between cuts.
• Establishing a start ID before the beginning of each cut.
• Preparing a time log accurate to the second (which includes start time and end times).
• Sequencing: putting songs in the right order.
• Eliminating any sounds you do not want on the tape, such as unnecessary noises between cuts.
• Eliminating any tunes you do not want included.

Converting your tape to a suitable format and sampling rate. DAT is the most acceptable format; 44.1 kHz the most acceptable sampling rate.

Your time log (or take sheet) needs to indicate not only accurate running times but any EQ variance that you're aware of from one cut to another. You'll also need to indicate whether you want to fade to black or have ambient sound between cuts.

Your tape needs to have calibration tones. And if it has been run through noise reduction, it requires that specific noise reduction tone. The specific type of noise reduction used must be indicated on your time log.

Your tape needs enough leader (15 seconds of blank tape) at the head, as well as an equal amount of tail (pre-roll and post-roll). Each cut needs a start ID. There needs to be enough time between cuts (3 to 5 seconds), and typically, that time should be uniform throughout.

Everything not wanted in the final product must be eliminated *before* sending it to be mastered. All false starts, outtakes, superfluous notes, sounds or noises between cuts, and unwanted cuts should be edited out. If it's not going to be on the final product, do not submit it to the mastering engineer.

These days, most recording is submitted for mastering on DAT, but if you're sending an analog master on an open reel, the tape needs to be prepared properly for shipping—with enough leader (several feet at both the beginning and the end), slow wound, tail out, boxed and labeled properly (identifying it as audiotape), with the time log and any other requested information enclosed.

If you'll be converting A/D, the industry standard (and the sampling rate to produce CDs) is 44.1 kHz. Are all the tunes recorded at the same sampling rate? If different cuts were recorded on different machines, this might not be the case. If anything has been done outside the studio, at home, for example, the sampling rate of those parts may be 48 kHz. That will require some work in mastering. Some people have told me it can't be done. Others that it can, but conversion from 48 to 44.1 kHz is a multistep process that can be extremely costly to the quality (to the pocketbook too). If you have any such tunes, you might seriously consider scrapping them rather than become entangled in conversion.

Have all of these issues attended to before you send your tape off to be mastered. Any postproduction adjustments that need to be made by the mastering lab will be charged to you.

Be aware that DAT tape typically has a high error rate at the beginning. Thirty seconds of black is recommended at the head. Write down any anomaly you may be aware of. If any given track needs more treble, make a note of it. If a passage seems too thin, make a note of it. Give the lab an accurate indication of the time at which such problems occur.

It's important to listen to your tape after any conversion for problems that the conversion itself may have caused. Remember that digital conversions lend themselves to playback at what seems to be very low amplitude. If you're supplying analog tape, is the overall level what you want? You might take one from the professionals' play book and listen to your tape played loud on a set of cheapo speakers to see how well it holds. Play it at lower volumes as well to see how it holds.

If the mastering engineer needs to use compression or limiters in order to get the sound loud enough or to suppress an analog tape that's too hot, you'll be charged for those remedies. It's easier all around, and cheaper too, to provide the tape ready to go, with strict observance of the mastering lab's requirements. Ask your engineer to look at the literature the mastering lab provides. Save a few bucks, avoid surprises, do it right, give them what they ask for.*

Just as tracking and mixing are two distinct processes, each demanding a particular focus, mixing and mastering are distinct processes. The common wisdom is that it is an extremely rare person who can mix *and* master. And no one should mix and master the same tape. Professionals send their tapes out to be mastered, and so should you.

When it comes to mastering, you want a person who is trained specifically for that task, is dedicated strictly to that task, and has facilities with the finest processors built for that task. Studio tracking processors are not built for mastering. At this point in the game, you've put in many hours of hard work getting the best you can on tape. The engineer has done whatever is possible to record it well and to mix it and make the orchestration strong. This is not the time to

---

* I recommend that you call Disc Makers at 800-468-8353 and ask about their *Guide to Master Tape Preparation* if you are interested in an in-depth discussion of this matter.

start scrimping on either time or money. You don't want to risk everything you've done. Good music, properly recorded and nicely mixed, demands to be mastered correctly.

MASTERING DEFINED

Mastering is apparently an enigma. Many amateur artists don't see the need for it. Others simply have their mix mastered flat (as is). But it's no wonder that artists have no understanding of the importance of mastering. Many people in the studio end of things seem to be at a loss to explain the process. When they do, the term *tweaked* is thrown around a great deal—although what is being tweaked, or why it demands tweaking, is never made entirely clear. They describe the process in vague terms, as though it were some kind of alchemy.

There really is no mystery to mastering. Mastering is the absolutely critical, rather precise process through which your tape is prepared for production. Technically, each format has specific requirements to create a master from which copies can be made. Part of mastering is seeing that those technical requirements are met.

Mastering is also one final chance to catch problems, to edit out mistakes, to drive the volume up (optimizing levels), to adjust the overall EQ, and to generally consolidate the individual cuts into a whole. Since each cut has been handled separately (recorded and mixed individually), there can be quite a diversity between cuts in terms of EQ and levels. In mastering, that's corrected.

Problems that may have occurred in conversion and gone undetected are taken care of. All of the things that should have been done in preparing your tape for mastering are checked. If they haven't been done, or they've been done incorrectly, they're taken care of or fixed. For this purpose your mix-down is transferred to a digital editor, where sequencing is checked; time between cuts is checked and adjusted; the beginning and end of each cut is adjusted (fade to black, ambient sound, or cross-fade into the next cut); and buzzes, clicks, pops, lip smacks, hissing sounds, and popping Ps are all attended to.

Mastering is, in fact, the last chance to do some tweaking. It's the point at which sweetening is optimally enhanced to get clarity, brilliance, sparkle, and punch. It's the point at which EQ is adjusted to lock in depth, warmth, and smoothness. It's the point at which compression can drive your recording up to "essential competitive levels." Done well, mastering, through such attention, can turn baser recordings into gold. Suffice it to say that every tune released by every major label is always mastered.

The question arises, "Didn't all this stuff get done in the mix?" The answer is, in the mix your tape was prepared for mastering. In mastering, your tape is prepared for duplication. The finished tracks are converted to the appropriate medium for duplication. DAT is used for producing cassettes; 3/4-inch tape for CDs. And a reference copy is sent to you.

When looking into having your tape mastered, don't forget to ask about turnaround time. Mastering isn't anything you want to rush—and most people involved in this end of the process won't be pushed—but you'll want to know. If they tell you it will take three weeks, mark your calendar four weeks down the road. That way, you'll be pleasantly surprised if you get the stuff back before the calendar date. If you climb on the phone before the promised date, you'll only be setting yourself up for indifference, bland explanations, disappointment, and frustration.

THE MASTERING ENGINEER'S TASK

Unless mastering is something that interests you a great deal, or if the sound you're after is very subtle and you don't think they'll get it, you should leave mastering to the experts. It requires more than just a subtle ear; it requires highly honed technical skills as well. Unless you're offered the unique opportunity to sit in, stay out of it entirely, except for approval.

While working on the project, you've heard the tunes so many times that, by the time you've finished editing, it will be almost impossible to keep the necessary analytical perspective. Things that you intended to correct might have been forgotten; some problems sound so familiar that they go undetected or you start to take a liking to them. It's difficult to pay attention to details and at the same time see the overall presentation. So the mastering engineer's perspective is invaluable.

This expert hasn't heard your work a thousand times, is not personally involved in your project, and therefore offers purely objective ears. Maintaining a critical view, the mastering engineer listens for aesthetics as well as technical flaws, catches any mistakes that may have been overlooked or forgotten, and makes all necessary corrections. Throughout this process the overall presentation is carefully considered. This may sound like a lot of change, but don't worry. The only changes in your finished tape should be improvement.

Do not be surprised if the tape you're offered for approval sounds different from what you expected. The mastering engineer was not involved in the project earlier and therefore may not know exactly what kind of sound you're after. You may need to explain it. If you can arrange to talk to the engineer before the mastering gets underway, that can help.

THE MASTERING ENGINEER

Mastering engineer is a very different breed of engineer. The job of this person is to make fine adjustments to your mix that have permanent aesthetic and commercial repercussions. So it behooves you to go with the best person available. A good mastering engineer can actually save a bad tape.

Some upstart and lesser-known mastering engineers, in an effort to demonstrate their skills and get their name out there, are willing to master one cut for you at a very low price. They'll shoot you a tape or CD with your original tune back to back with their mastered version so you can compare them. These people usually also offer a very good price on mastering your entire project, so ask about a flat-rate package. They have to be competitively priced to survive. The only thing such an experiment will cost you is a little time. If you're anxious to get things finished, ask about turnaround time when you contact these people. Turnaround is another area where the smaller guy can really compete. The big lab may not be able, or even willing, to give you the special consideration that the smaller one can.

Some so-called mastering engineers set themselves up by buying a computer program designed to master tapes. But beware, a great recording can be butchered in mastering. A mastering engineer is much more than a technician with a computer program. Such programs, in the hands of a knowledgeable person, can be fine. It pays to find someone whose specialty is mastering and who has a studio set up strictly for that task. Do not risk everything you've done by trying to save a few bucks.

How do you differentiate between those who know what they're doing and those who don't? Reputation. Ask around. Make a few phone calls. Ask at the studio where you did your recording. They want a certain quality about everything that comes from their studio. They want their work on your tape to sound great. They should be able to refer you to a good mastering engineer.

From what I've been told, in the entire country there are only a handful of people who can master a tape the way it should be. Outrageous as that statement may sound, when I repeated it to engineers, sound technicians, and producers, they all pretty much agreed. (Maybe they each have a different handful in mind, though.) Apparently, the best mastering engineers all work out of L.A. and do not charge much more than people who might not know what they're doing. If you're referred to someone in L.A., you may have to wait a few months. It's worth the wait to have your good hard work properly mastered.

We're told that tape manufacturers that offer complete mastering/replication packages "do a pretty good job." You just send them a DAT tape and a photograph, and they master it, manufacture it, package it, and ship it to you in a few weeks. Some of them do everything from layout and design of the cover to liner notes. If you go with one of these organizations, your tape will certainly look professional.

Dale Miller talks about the process:

> I went to Fantasy to work with George Horn—legendary mastering engineer—and I took my recording engineer with me. And, man, it's an experience. . . . They started talking this stuff that was way beyond me. But I loved it. My recording engineer tweaked the sound with George, and they got a much better sound. I thought it was much better. And I knew *I* couldn't have done it. Mastering is pretty advanced stuff. I guess if you have a recording engineer you really like, or if you have a really good ear and feel competent, you can go in. But mastering's tough. If you go to a major mas-

tering studio, you're paying $200 per hour. It was worth it for me. If you're on a budget, I guess that's something you could skip. But working with people who really know what they're doing is very enjoyable.

And the results are worth the price. The music industry professionals you hope will hear your tape are discerning and have certain expectations when it comes to sound quality. Mastering makes a good recording into a better recording, and a better recording into something that will make 'em sit up in their chairs and maybe even stop picking their teeth. Give 'em you're best shot and you won't regret it. Anything less and you will.

CHECKING THE REFERENCE COPY FOR APPROVAL

The mastering lab will provide a reference copy (a dub) of what they've done for your approval. You need to get together with your producer and listen to this reference copy. The mastering lab needs your formal approval. If they'll also be manufacturing the finished product, they'll need your approval before production begins. Listen to these tapes carefully, more than once. This is your *last* chance to catch anything you may not want on your final product.

If, after listening to the reference copy, you want additional, minor changes, they shouldn't cost you anything more. (Of course, if you're changing the entire product, that's a different story.) The settings that were used to master your tape are all recorded, so dialing in on them again is quick, reliable, and accurate. If anyone says anything to you about "setup time" at this point in the game, it's a rip-off. Make it clear that you know better, but always be kind to anyone who has possession of your master tape—at least until you get it back.

DUPLICATION

There are technical considerations depending upon what method of duplication (or replication or manufacturing) you choose. With the return of vinyl, 2X, real-time, and half-speed mastering may need to be considered. Half-speed is the best (and most expensive); 2X the cheapest. That should be enough information for you to decide.

High-speed duplication is the most common method used to produce cassette tapes, but it benefits manufacturers only. They want to get those tapes in and out of the shop. People who do this work claim that there is little or no loss between replicating your master tape in real time or 16 times the speed at which it is normally played. In most high-speed operations, the mastered tape is looped so that it plays through and then begins again while a long roll of continuous tape zips by, copying the signal. Later it's cut to length and loaded into cassettes. In other methods the tape is preloaded into the cassette, and each is then recorded individually, in real time. Naturally, one of these methods is more expensive. You decide.

The quality of the mechanism you have your music done on is important. A good-quality cassette is helpful in many ways. People in the industry unanimously advise that you use the best-quality tape you can afford. Although many labels do not follow such advice themselves, most listeners can hear the difference, not to mention the noise cheap cassettes generate while playing. Almost everyone has experienced the mechanical failure of such tapes. It's also important to recall that some people in the Biz simply look at a tape to determine if it's worth listening to. If a better cassette might get you a listen, it's worth a few extra bucks.

Noise reduction can cause problems both in recording and in duplication. Common wisdom says it shouldn't be used at all in duplication unless you go to the finest, most expensive facilities—which are set up to use noise reduction properly, without mistakes.

This may appear to be simplistic, but *always,* always listen to each promo (or pitch) tape you plan to send out. Whether it's serving as an audition or going to a label, a defective tape may be the end of any chance you may have had otherwise. Start at the beginning of the tape and listen to the entire first cut. If there's no problem at the beginning, it's unlikely to show up later. Personally, I'd listen to the rest anyway. What you're looking for are flaws created by a bad recording head on the machine that made that particular tape. If you don't listen to each tape, such a simple matter could be the cause for a rejection and you might never know it.

Also, if you're going to be shooting tapes to people, make sure each tape is wound and ready to go. You want it set up so there is maybe a second, but not much more, between pushing that play button and being enthralled by that first magnificent note.

9

THE INDUSTRY

MUSICIANS LIKE TO BELIEVE that the music industry is about music. It is not. If it's about anything, it's about marketing. The eyes of most industry executives remain lifeless and flat as long as you're talking about music. The word *business* sometimes kindles the spark of life. Mention *units shipped,* and you might detect a twitching about the eyes. Talk about *units sold,* and you set their little hardened hearts aflutter.

The music business is run by hard-headed businesspeople, admittedly self-serving types with strong instincts for what is commercially viable and what can be marketed to the record-buying public. The fact that it's music that these businesspeople are dealing in is almost beside the point. If selling shoes were as lucrative as selling records, they'd all be selling shoes, and we'd all probably be buying them, whether we needed more shoes or not.

Van Morrison put it neatly: "Music is spiritual. The music business is not." More precisely, music is spiritual to the epicureans among us. The marketplace, however, is full of ravenous hedonists—on both sides of the counter. One of the secrets the record execs know is that the consumer doesn't understand, or even care to understand, music. They do understand things like image, hype, showmanship. Their musical knowledge is confined to volume, beat, and rhythm, probably in that order. The lyrics to a song seem to mean a lot, and people yearn to believe they apply personally to their lives. These are the things the music business offers the record buyer. Of course, it's easier for musicians if they believe otherwise.

The music business, boiled down to its residue, is just that—business. And like any other business, it has no heart. Musicians commonly make a mistake thinking that it does. The music industry is about obtaining the rights to songs and exploiting those rights commercially to the fullest extent possible. It's also about creating an ever-emerging onslaught of new talent so that new material is continually available to an unpredictable, somewhat mindless, but apparently insatiable market.

Look at what happens to a song after it's written. From there it's transcribed, copyrighted, and published. It's made into a demo. It's peddled by a lawyer or publisher. Through contacts and with hard work, persuasion, and an unfair portion of good luck, someone with a contract likes it, considers it. From there, if the luck continues, it will be selected, worked on, routined, rehearsed, and taken into the studio. Once recorded, if it's selected to remain part of the set, it's edited, mastered, pressed, packaged, promoted, distributed, and sold. Someone, somewhere, tracks the sales and works out the royalties. If it gets airplay, someone keeps an eye on that. Another eye is kept on those who might perform it on stage. Fees are collected, royalties distributed. In short: *everything* that happens to that song once it leaves the songwriter is business. All of it. Little of it has to do with music.

The process involves negotiations and contracts and phone calls and luncheons and leverage and figures and percentages and mountains and mountains of paperwork. These are all business transactions. They require licensing organizations, unions, herds of lawyers, entire teams of promotional people, publishers and publicists, personal and business managers, writers, studio musicians, distributors, retailers, bookkeepers, administrators, secretaries, and countless drones at every level. All of them are businesspeople. The decisions they make about that tune are business decisions. Each and every one of them is dealing in a product. The product happens to be music, but to them music is business.

Charlie Musselwhite notes:

> In addition to that, I don't know if it's a secret or not, but there are a lot of people out there who are waiting to screw you. Maybe some of them don't even mean to. They might mean the best, but their idea of how things should go often turns out to be wrong. You just have to be careful. It's just like anything else, you know, you have to follow your instincts—and *they* can often be wrong too. Nobody really has a handle on it. Even people who have been in the business for a long time. Everybody's got their own ideas. It's really a crap shoot, all the time, every minute. You never know what's gonna work and what is not gonna work.

Whether publisher, agent, producer, or just some guy with the bucks, they're all there to exploit the music to the fullest extent possible and not necessarily to your benefit. Every person who pretends to be your friend or happy to see you is not necessarily your friend. They may, however, be very happy to see you.

How doth the little crocodile improve his shining tail,
And pour the waters of the Nile, on every golden scale.
How cheerfully he seems to grin, how neatly spreads his claws,
And welcomes little fishes in, with gently smiling jaws.

—LEWIS CARROLL

Too many artists think that because it has to do with music, they can be casual about the business end of things. Nothing could be further from the truth. Anyone you work with or for can help you into a tight situation. Most of them will be glad to do it. Some do it unwittingly while doing you a favor. With that revelation in place, let's take another look at demos.

THE DAYDREAM

You've gone into the studio, and after the efforts of Sisyphus, you've emerged with an outstanding tape. *Everyone* knows it's great. The studio staff told you so while patting you on the back and urging you to come back again soon. Your friends and relatives all agree. By declension, you yourself now know that destiny has you slated to become a recording artist. It's just a matter of getting a label to recognize this undeniable fact.

But you're not worried because you've got an up-to-date mailing list. You've planned ahead. Preparation, printing, and shipping of a hot promo package are all part of your budget. So you've laid the budgetary foundation necessary to support your monumental talent.

The imagined scenario plays out like this: Some legitimate guy in the Biz (not some weasel) finds your package on his desk. He's curious enough to open it up. The cassette is good quality, the labeling nicely done. A glance confirms that there are only three tunes on there and none of them will take too much of his time. He looks at your photo and thinks the kids can probably relate to the way you look. He plunks it in the machine. Then he leans back in his split-calfskin leather chair, locks his manicured fingers behind his closely cropped, thinning, nicely graying head and closes his bloodshot eyes. Since this is your daydream, he listens to your demo carefully from beginning to end. At no time during the process is he distracted by the demands of running a record company. The phone doesn't ring, no one walks into his office, his mind doesn't drift on to other matters. He listens, uninterrupted, to your tape.

Then he jumps out of his seat, screaming, "We gotta get this kid on our roster!" He snatches up the phone and screams at his assistant to track you down and deliver you forthwith to headquarters in a limousine. Meanwhile, he calls everyone else on staff into his office to admire your undeniable genius. What else could he do? You've given him the best damned music you can make, and he's clever enough to recognize it. After all, that's his business.

Quite frankly, *you* know (don't you?) that most labels don't recognize great music when they hear it. Some of them just don't have the ear for it. Some of them don't care. More to the point, great music is not really what they're looking for. Despite the cherished myth that industry executives are eagerly pawing through stacks of tapes each day, desperate to find the next superstar to add to their roster, the fact is that most record industry executives rarely have time to listen to tapes. Most industry execs *are not* sitting around waiting for your tape to arrive; they're busy working on things they've already got going.

But all you need to do is reach *that one guy.* You're just looking for that one visionary who has an ear for your music. Then you're in. All you have to do is to get your tape to that person. Unfortunately, most of the people in the Biz who can do your career any good have an entire staff of people whose sole purpose is to keep that from happening. Their job is to look blandly at incoming material, yawn or smirk or laugh or shrug, and then toss it casually into an already over-flowing garbage can and thus spare the boss the effort. When it comes to the record biz, the always insightful Frank Zappa nailed it succinctly: "If you're not cynical about the situation, then, obviously, you're not very well informed about the situation." Frank may have said this about life in America in general, but it suits the record industry perfectly.

Let's be honest about this for just a moment. If your dream is to become a recording artist, you should look carefully at why so many people in satellite and peripheral businesses *used to* have that same dream. There is a reason why you can walk into any music shop in America and find a person behind the counter who can casually lay out a beautiful little "Maple Leaf Rag" after slapping on a set of new strings for you. There's a reason the repair guy can check his work-manship by nicking out anything from a Scarlatti scherzo to a pulsing, pounding "Purple Haze." There's a reason why they all wear that knowing grin when you stroll in chattering animatedly about your recent stint in the studio. And there's a reason why they roll their eyes when you mention desire. They may know some-thing you don't about the Biz.

One of the things they may know—and probably empirically—is that dupli-cating your demo tape in order to shoot it to industry execs is like buying a Lamborghini. It's largely an ego-based decision; it's extremely costly; and in the end, you're either going to find yourself out there stuck in traffic along with everybody else or with the somewhat embarrassing evidence of your foolhardy venture sitting around rotting under a tarp in your garage.

But you can't slight the Lamborghini dealer for selling you the car. And you can't slight tape manufacturers for giving you a very good price on 500 or 1,000 or 5,000 copies of your tape. They may say it's their job to support your dream, but their *real* job is to accept your money. You certainly can't blame the record-ing studio for giving you the very best ammunition for your pop gun so you can go out there and stalk the big game.

At some juncture you may start to feel resentful because you went to such great expense and were never given a real chance. The road to hell is paved with the discarded bitter souls of musicians who felt like they never got the chance they deserved. It's a legitimate gripe. The fact is, they probably didn't. Unfortunately, despite the myth that, if you just keep plugging, sooner or later (sooner in California, later elsewhere) you'll end up smug and rich and living off royalties, it's many times more likely that you'll spend your entire career pump-ing out the very best you have to offer and wind up pretty much where you start-ed. That's if you're aggressively lucky.

It's easy to see why musicians who have plugged and tugged and shoved and crammed and hammered and slipped and skidded and crashed and burned and picked themselves up, just to wade in again—swimming out there all alone, way out in the deep water, in way over their heads (surrounded by sharks and leeches of every sort) and clinging only to the barely buoyant sliver that hope alone provides—can think that the business is rotten from top to bottom. Somebody say hallelujah. Because they know that on some fine, sunny island, far lesser talents are lying around in the shade of coconut trees, sipping Mai Tai's delivered by beer commercial blondes. Meanwhile, back out there in the cold, wet, all alone, tossing endlessly between a relentless blistering sun and the chilling bitterness of eternal night, they continue the struggle just to stay afloat.

No matter what you've been told. No matter what you need to believe in order to get by, whether you make it or not has nothing to do with talent. Talent doesn't count because, whatever the music industry is about, it certainly ain't about talent. Besides, everybody's got talent. It's prerequisite. In fact, at times real talent can get in the way of your career. Sugar-Pie DeSanto comes to mind.

Sugar-Pie DeSanto could always dance and sing with the best of them. When she and Etta James were young girls growing up together, they used to blow the minds of everyone who ever saw them perform. Because Sugar-Pie was such a wonderful entertainer, a very famous artist hired her, thinking she'd add to his show. But that was precisely the problem. Maybe Sugar-Pie added a little too much to the show. When this VFA would shout and jump into the air, Sugar-Pie would shout louder and jump up higher. If he jumped up and spun around two times, Sugar-Pie jumped up and spun around three times. If he jumped up, spun around three times, and landed in a split, Sugar-Pie jumped up, spun around four times, and landed in a split, doing the funky dog.

Naturally, the audience loved it. The famous artist, on the other hand, was not so entertained. It was beginning to look like they'd have to rename the tour The Sugar-Pie DeSanto Show, with good-old-what's-his-name added. So Sugar-Pie was moved out. So much for talent. Sugar-Pie's talent cost her that gig.

A FEW KIND WORDS

Historically speaking, the record labels don't always come out looking so good. The stories of labels giving some naïve young artist the keys to a Cadillac in exchange for the rights to all of his songs are literally true. The problem, however, is that without the record companies, many of those early artists would not have gotten anything for their songs. In the ongoing and bitter criticism of the industry, artists fail to recognize the plain pie-in-the-face fact that without the labels there would be no royalties.

One time I was sitting around with bluesman Chester D. Wilson (who has been on this planet since 1915). I was ranting on about how this European label was trying to screw a local musician. The label had reported to him that his album wasn't selling very well in Europe, while a friend coming back from the continent showed him a trade publication that suggested the thang was selling through the roof. While I ranted on about this, Chester just sat there listening, and when I finally wound down, he said quietly, "Well, Richard, everything you say is true. But where would we be without them?"

That's the point. Whether a record label was formed out of the pure love of the music—as were Delmark, Alligator, and Arhoolie—or formed by some wiseguy recently yanked up the evolutionary scale through connections, without them there would be no dream. For huge segments of society there would be no music at all.

By the way, royalty reform measures have been launched by several major labels to compensate artists who may have been taken advantage of in earlier years. They've not only upped the royalty rate but also forgiven unrecouped balances that such artists might have owed the labels.

A TRUE STORY

A dozen years ago a country singer was invited to the executive offices of a major record label. He'd been playing around L.A. for so long and to such large crowds that he could no longer be ignored. When he walked in, the executive behind the desk did an abnormally courteous thing for someone in the Biz—he actually looked up from whatever he was doing. Then he said in a surly tone, "I'm eatin' lunch here." As if to illustrate the fact, he took a huge chomp out of a big fat sandwich. A classic record industry welcome.

The country singer ignored the rudeness, stepped forward and dropped a heavy stack of papers on the exec's desk. It landed with a resounding thud. The exec looked at the papers, snorted derisively, then chortled, "What the hell is that?" When the kid told him what it was, things changed. The executive put down his sandwich, sat up in his chair, snatched up the phone, and barked orders to get one of the label's 10,000 lawyers in there right away. From that moment on, the meeting became downright genteel. Thereafter the country singer was treated very nicely. After a couple of hours of negotiations, he was signed. For the record, he has proven to be one of the leading record sellers in the industry.

"Wow," I hear you say. "What was that stack of paper? What could possibly be powerful enough to cause a record industry executive to put down a sandwich and start treating an unsigned artist like a human being?" I know this is what you're thinking because that's the very same thought that crossed my mind when I first heard this story. [Insert pregnant pause here.] It was a mailing list. According to some, it had half a million names and addresses on it; according to others, a mere 100,000. Either way, in the mind of the industry executive, that list translated rapidly, and naturally, into percentage/units sold.

Note that the singer did not go in saying what a great singer he was. And notice too that demo tapes have nothing to do with the story. The industry exec hadn't heard a demo of this singer, although admittedly he had heard his name around town for years. The artist didn't attempt to prove his abilities as a performer; he *did,* however, demonstrate his marketability. In short, he spoke the language.

If you want to get the attention of music industry execs, you have to speak their language. One way is to go that same route. Get in the door toting the names of 100,000 fans who have already bought your music. It's a proven effective method. If you can get in there and spout enthusiastically about demographics, market share, raising the floor on the MAP for front-line product, box-lot cost (the defensive view), mainstream markets, multiple markets, or anything having to do with vertical integration without actually mentioning vertical integration, it couldn't hurt you.

The industry is always looking for new talent, of course. Helping new talent reach its full potential is their avowed business. But talent's full potential is not an aesthetic goal. Talent's full potential is measured in first-week totals, global exposure, a broadening fan base, cross-over appeal, staying power. And all of those things are really synonyms for sales. The delight you see written on the faces of label execs when they see a bullet on the charts is not based on any interest in music per se. The charts do not track music; the charts track sales.

Naturally, the labels are interested in anyone who might grind out a hit single or two for them. But make no mistake about it, the Biz eyes musicians the same way pubescent boys glom young girls—*and* with pretty much the same intentions. Whatever else you may want to believe, signing with a label does not mean they've invested in your long-term career. Just because they buy you, right off, with a fifty-dollar handshake doesn't mean they'll lend you a hand if you stumble. If you stumble, there are ten thousand others eager to take your place. And it's a rare label that will either stop or stoop to pick you up. The cold view is this: dumping talent helps to balance the books. If they put money into you and it doesn't pay off, for you it may be the end of your career, but for them it's a write-off.

Here's some real information: *Timing is everything.* This has been confirmed by musicians and label execs alike. When I asked Robben Ford what separated him out from other, equally talented, but less successful guitarists, he replied: "Well, you know, 'right place at the right time' has a *lot* to do with it."

Charlie Musselwhite has this to say:

> You know, there are a lot of great musicians out there that nobody will ever know of. And there's probably a lot of great music out there that will never be recorded. Somebody said talent is only about 10 percent of the business. The rest of it is who you know and being in the right place at the right time. That's why a lot of people live in L.A. or New York. If you're living somewhere in South Dakota, you're not going to get the call. They're gonna call the guy that lives around the corner, that's maybe not as good as you, but they know can do the job that minute.

What is rarely understood by musicians is that record label executives have very strict ideas about what is of interest to them, and they never cross the line to consider anything that is not. Neither do they have the time to refer you to others. If you are the greatest horn player in the world, and you present yourself to an industry exec whose twin brother is desperately looking for a horn player, the exec will turn you away. One of the reasons these people are so good at what they do is, they're looking for something in particular and they are not easily distracted.

It's not at all unusual to shoot a tape to someone in the Biz, only to hear back, "Yeah, I gave it a listen. They're great. I played it for a couple of the other people here. They think they're great too. Real tasty stuff. The piano is remarkable. The vocalist is a standout. They look good; they sound good. Fantastic horn section. A unique sound. We even like the name of the band. It's not anything we'd be interested in." Believe me, when people in the Biz spout that kind of verbiage, they mean every word of it. They did actually listen. They did think the band was great. They did play it for the other execs, and they, too, thought the band was great. Typically, "It's not anything we'd be interested in" is the first and only thing out of their mouths.

Of course, for the artist this kind of response is confusing. If they thought it was so good, why did they pass on it? The answer to this riddle is simple: If you don't give them what they're after, they're not interested. It doesn't matter how great it is. That's reality. There is a lot to be said for the common wisdom about studying a label's roster and listening to the music they've already put out. If your stuff is a perfect fit with everything else they've got going, you have a very good chance—assuming you can get to them to let them know about this perfect fit

At any given moment, on any given week, industry execs may have something very specific in mind, and anything else—no matter how good—is not even considered. If you don't meet the current criteria, they're simply not interested. I've been told directly by people in the Biz that if you offer them something they were interested in last week, you're too late. If you offer them something they may be interested in next week, by the time they get to it, you've probably been forgotten. If you get your tape into the hands of the right person at precisely the right moment, you're in. If you get the same tape to the same person working on anything else, you haven't got a chance.

What that means to you is shoot them your stuff again, even if they've rejected you before. And if they've rejected your old stuff, shoot them your new stuff. Maybe they thought you were close last time. Call them up first and make arrangements so they'll be looking for your tape.

When I was a kid, we used to trade useless trinkets in the schoolyard before classes began. If another kid had something you wanted, you'd make him an offer. If he liked the deal, you'd swap junk and both walk away drooling with success. One morning a kid showed up at school with a broken pocketwatch that was about the coolest thing I'd ever seen. I asked him if he wanted to trade. He said,

"Maybe." I offered him marbles and tin soldiers and Indian-head pennies and some other neat stuff. He said, "Nuh," and started to walk. I ran after him and offered him my rabbit's foot. But he continued to walk away from the deal. I yelled after him, "How about my cap gun *and* a water pistol?"—he kept walking—"*and* my best shooter?" He stopped, turned, thought, "Nuh." That was my best offer. It was practically everything I owned.

The next morning another kid had that broken pocketwatch. He was proudly showing it around before school. "Man, how did you get it?" I asked with envy. He shrugged, "Traded for it."

"Yeah, but what'd you give him? I offered him everything I own." It turned out that he'd traded him a little paper American flag. I couldn't believe it. I had, like, three or four of those little American flags, but it never occurred to me that the kid with the watch would be interested in them.

That's the way the record industry works. Give them what they want, and you get the broken pocketwatch. Offer them anything else, and some other kid with a lot less to offer gets the broken watch.

A LITTLE CLOSER LOOK AT THE SIGNED ARTIST

The best-kept secret in the industry is that even the biggest stars can, and often do, sell hundreds of thousands of units and still end up owing the label money. That's because, with advances, cross-collateralization, and multi-album deals, the label may not recoup until the term of the contract is about to run out—some contracts are designed that way. In cross-collateralization, royalties due on an album are withheld until all the label's costs are recouped on other albums. That doesn't mean money isn't coming in; it only means, for accounting purposes, no profit has been made.

The industry is set up and contracts are written to ensure that the label will eventually recover every dollar spent and take the lion's share of the profits as well. There is no assurance, of any sort, that the artist will ever see a penny. In fact, in many cases there's no assurance that a record will even be produced. It is entirely possible to be signed, go into the studio, produce a master, owe the label money, without an album ever being pressed.

If not clever and cautious, the artist can actually end up in the position where every unit sold increases the debt; a case in which the more successful the album is, the less hope there is of the artist ever recovering financially. Meanwhile, everyone else is making money on the arrangement. That's the plan. The industry is designed to make the record company rich; it is not designed to make the performer rich. "I want you kids to learn how to share" is not something the mothers of industry execs ever taught them.

For a truly frightening look into the problems a signed artist can become entangled in, check out *All You Need to Know about the Music Business* by Donald S. Passman (Prentice Hall, 1991). He'll walk you through some eye-opening horror stories.

If you sign with a label, that does not mean they're on your side. It only means they are willing to put their weight behind your product in return for an agreed-upon share of the profits. Just to be clear, though, they aren't doing that for you; they're doing it for themselves, for the label. Most record contracts are basically nothing more or less than an employment agreement. You're working for the label. In most cases they tell you what songs to do, when and where you're going to do them, and how you're going to do them. That's why a band that has been touring for years and gathering an enthusiastic following will get picked up by a label and make an album of music that is nothing at all like the stuff that got them there.

RECORD DEALS

A record deal is not the ultimate goal; a record deal is just the beginning of your education about the music industry. Signing with a label can actually mean the end of your career. If you do not prove yourself productive, or you do not move enough product, or you're the least bit unmanageable, you may find yourself dropped from the roster. Once dropped, you'll probably find that it's harder to get signed again than it was to get signed in the first place.

Worse than being dropped, of course, is finding yourself signed to a record label that doesn't give you tour support or make any effort to get your songs air-play. If you look at the list of artists on any label's roster and then count up the ones you've actually heard from, that'll give you some idea of how common this is. Some artists find themselves locked into a contract with a label that makes no efforts on their behalf yet won't release them to sign with anyone else. They are forced to produce albums just to fulfill a contract. In order to escape from a label that they can't work with, they go into the studio and bitterly grind out tunes they do not want to do, on albums that they're not eager to make. This is probably not the scenario they envisioned while putting pen to paper at the joyous contract signing.

Moon Zappa was the prize one time on an L.A.-based TV dating game. Three young studs were hoping to win her. When the first guy came jaunting out, all muscles and irrepressible self-approval, Moon looked him right in the eye and asked, "Tell me how you feel about back acne, excessive body hair, and cellulite." The guy's jaw dropped; his eyes bugged out; he was knocked senseless. TKO. Nothing could have prepared him for this. He'd imagined himself dashing out to meet some bimbo with a question that began, "If I was a muffin, and you were a big hungry bear . . ." The guy just sat there gaping until the hostess revived him, helped him up onto his feet, and sent him stumbling off stage. On his way out, he was still so stunned that he staggered, face first, into one of the cameras.

Moon's point was "If you can't face reality, then we don't even need to talk." It was made as cleanly and decisively as any point in all of TV dating game history. Unwittingly, Frank's daughter offered, I think, very good advice to anyone aspiring to deal with the record industry. A record contract is not a dream date. Whatever the beauty of its trappings, unveiled, the industry is riddled with back acne and excessive body hair and cellulite. From personal experience I can tell you it also has bad breath. Until you're prepared to face that reality, you're only fooling yourself. Watch the camera on your way out.

ROYALTY REALITY

Consider this: The big-time rock star can make 12 percent of the retail price on units sold. First, however, that price is reduced by anywhere from 10 percent (tapes) to 25 percent (CDs) to cover the cost of packaging. So the figure that the star is getting 12 percent of has diminished. Payments are made semiannually on 90 percent of units sold, *after* recoupment, and from 30 to 40 percent of that may be held in reserve (meaning, it's not to be paid yet—maybe sometime later—we'll think about it).

Semiannually means that, in between, you may be drawing further advances in order to survive. Recoupment means that the recovery of any and all advances and the cost of recording come out of your royalties. Recoupment also means the label recovers their costs before the artist gets a cent. Your royalties are based on only 90 percent of units sold because, sometime around the dawn of history, records used to be fragile, breakable things. Back then, 10 percent of them didn't make it through the hazards of distribution. Back then, the record companies shrugged and said to the retailer, "Hey, don't worry about it. It's understandable that some get broken. So just pay us for 90 percent of them." Naturally, if the record company was being paid for only 90 percent of units sold, they weren't going to turn around and pay the artist for 100 percent of units sold. So even today the artist gets royalties on 90 percent of units sold. And, as said, 30 percent or more may be held in reserve against possible returns. Many times, through the magic of creative bookkeeping, advances, and multi-album deals, the artist's share adds up to a whopping zero. Quite frequently, however, it adds up to a *huge,* impressive, even breathtaking figure . . . that the artist owes to the record label.

The producer's royalty usually comes directly from the artist's royalty too. Unlike your royalties, the producer's royalties start with the very first record sold. That means, before you've earned a cent, you already owe the producer some bucks. The producer has no responsibility for studio costs—that responsibility is solely yours. No royalties are paid on cut-outs (units no longer carried on the label's catalog or sold at reduced rates). Reduced-rate royalties are paid on every copy that goes to anywhere other than a retail outlet—record clubs, military installations, schools, libraries. No royalty is paid for promotional copies, which they calculate to be another 10 percent, sometimes more, *of all units manufactured.* And royalties on CDs are usually lower than on LPs (at least as long as CDs make up most of the market).

Depending upon your contract, you may or may not be allowed to look at all of the bookkeeping that concerns your album—such particulars need to be stated in your contract going in. And almost every record deal states that after a certain period, if you haven't formally questioned their accounting, even if they've screwed you, you no longer have the right to take a look at the books.

Meanwhile, personal managers get anything from 10 to 20 percent of all of your earnings. As long as the manager is at the helm (and actually, in many cases, long after that person's departure), that money comes off the top of your record deal. In short, it's extremely simple for a signed recording artist to get into deep financial difficulties. For insightful examples of this sort of thing, I recommend reading *Breaking In To The Music Business* by Alan H. Siegel (New York: Fireside Books, 1990). Read pages 19 through 22 for starters. After that, you'll want to read the rest.

ALTERNATE ROUTES

Unless you're overwhelmed with the desire to be batted around and gnawed on by the labels—before they move on to maul someone new—there are easier ways to make money with music. You might want to consider some. *Making Money Making Music (No Matter Where You Live)* by James Dearing offers many good alternatives. It's readable, convincing, and recommended. Even within the industry there are alternatives.

While it's almost impossible to fight your way into most labels and get anyone to listen to you, with determination it can be a bit easier to get to publishers, talent agents, and lawyers. It depends, of course, on what you have to offer, but that's one alternate route. What's attractive about this alternative is that, once you're signed with one of these people, they usually make serious efforts to promote your work, and the truly legit ones are connected and can make things happen.

A "pressing and distribution deal" can be a somewhat refreshing alternative. Basically, that means hiring a label's manufacturing and distribution arm to manufacture and ship your product. However, you need some real leverage (or real bucks) to make such an arrangement. The more common version is a distribution deal with an independent distributor. In that case you do the pressing and promotion, and they do the shipping. It's a straightforward deal, and royalties are typically almost the reverse of your normal record deal. In such an arrangement the people you're working with make no pretense of being invested in your career, which can be refreshing. But if you make an impressive accounting, it could lead to other things.

Another route is to get airplay for your demo on local radio stations. Some well-known performers have actually gotten their start by this method. You supply your favorite station with a CD (not a cassette) and beg them, face to face, one on one, to please, please, at least give it a listen. Getting to radio stations is not really any easier than getting to anyone else in the business. Nevertheless, many artists feel more comfortable approaching the program director at a station they listen to than trying to get to a record company exec. Depending upon your approach, it could happen. Many PDs enjoy being in the position to offer support to local talent.

The idea behind this kind of *micro-marketing* is that the proper response to airplay on one station will lead to other stations playing your tune. Growing interest will lead to affiliated stations in other areas picking it up. After it starts getting airplay regionally, and it looks like you're making a little money, the smell of blood gets in the water and draws the attention of bigger fish. If that happens, you may find yourself swimming around with independent promoters. These are people whose sole task is to get airplay for the labels they represent. They are highly skilled (and some say dangerous) professionals who know how to get what they want. Unfortunately, when people try to squeeze through the same door as the rep from LCN, it can be a tight squeeze, and occasionally somebody may get bruised.

PUBLISHING

If money's what you're interested in, the real money in the music business is not in performing but in publishing. The people who make the bucks are the songwriters, the lyricists, and the publishers. Many of the richest people in the industry are people whose names you may never have heard of and whose faces you'll never see. And if there is any part of the Biz where women can stand on their own, shoulder to shoulder with the boys, it's in songwriting.

In 1965 Curtis Mayfield had a good idea. Instead of generating big bucks for the record labels with his enormous talent, he decided to put a little money in his own pocket. He launched his own publishing company and held 100 percent of the rights. From that point on, if anyone wanted to use his material, they'd be paying him directly. Of course, Curtis Mayfield is not the only artist to make such a move. However, he was one of the first.

Since then, many recording artists, songwriters, and performers have made similar moves. If you sign with a label, you'll probably be asked to sign over half of the rights in a co-publishing deal—some labels demand as much before they'll add you to their roster. I am *not* suggesting that you refuse to negotiate these rights. It's normal procedure for performers to turn over publishing responsibilities to the label. But holding the publishing rights to your own work gives even the most inexperienced artist a little leverage when talking with the labels.

It is possible to be in the music business without getting entangled in the Biz. You can fulfill your dream of making a living as a musician, without offering yourself up as fodder for the cannons of the record industry. There is another use for what you've done in the studio that can actually make you some bucks. It's an option, in fact, that can bring in a pretty good return on your investment. From the outside, it may look deceptively small time.

WORKING MUSICIAN

I know a fingerpicker who bought himself a nice house in the Berkeley hills (where houses do not go cheap). He's not currently connected to any major label—in fact, he's always been tied to small independent labels—but he's doing pretty well. Unlike artists signed with major labels, his fans love him more than his accountant does. Instead of generating big bucks for some record label execs so they could live like royalty in Beverly Hills, he kept a few bucks and got a nice little home for himself.

He's a working musician. He has steady gigs and a steady following. Between sets his drummer or his wife sells tapes and t-shirts from a beaten-up old cardboard box at the corner of the stage. I guess anyone might call it small time. But putting your tape directly into the hands of people who enjoy your work is a solid career move. And there's another name for working 250 days a year in front of a growing, dedicated, enthusiastic following. Making a respectable living by playing your music for crowds of people who love what you're doing is sometimes called "success."

> **"If you're making a living playing music, you're beating out 99.9 percent of all aspiring musicians. Remember, you got into this for the music, not the fame."**
>
> —Bruce Iglauer, Alligator Records

A small-time working musician may make only a couple of hundred bucks a gig. But the musician can also make nine bucks on each tape sold. That's 75 percent of the retail price, or about 300 percent profit. Nothing taken off the top for breakage. The packaging has already been paid for. Nothing's held in reserve. The money goes directly from your fans to you. The real beauty of it is, you don't have to endure some accounting wizard presenting phony figures semiannually and whining about how difficult it is to make ends meet in a business that hauls down, annually, twice the income of all professional sports combined. There are certainly worse ways to make an honest living than playing gigs and selling your tapes directly to people who love your music.

CONCLUSION

WHATEVER YOU DO with the product of your hard work, going into the studio is guaranteed to be an adventure. If you've read this book and retained some of the information in it, then you have a very good shot at making your studio time productive, successful, and if not thoroughly enjoyable, at least understandable. You also have a pretty good shot at coming across in a professional manner while you're in there.

The difference between an upstart musician and a professional is that the professional knows all the stuff we've talked about here. If you take the time to prepare a budget, schedule your sessions, and find the right people to work with, if you prepare your instrument, yourself, and your music, you should come away with a quality product you can be proud of. The bonus is, you'll also find going in next time a lot easier.

If you're about to go in for the first time, you have a lot to look forward to. Once you get used to it, once you get hip to the process, once you settle down and it becomes OK, once you start "kickin' and cookin'," there's something rare and wonderful about recording your music. It's hard work, but it is also exhilarating. The compensation for your efforts is tremendous. Properly recorded, even tuning sounds good. Your music is bound to sound great.

Going into the professional recording studio for the first time is guaranteed to be one of the neatest things you'll ever do. It is certainly one of the most straightforward, uncluttered business arrangements you'll ever make in the music business.

Charlie Musselwhite wraps it up nicely, I think:

I've *always* loved bein' in the studio. I feel comfortable in the studio; it's fun and I love it. It's always been a pleasure to me. I've never frozen up or been uptight or nervous. To me it's relaxing. It's work. It's hard. It can be really tedious and tiresome, and it can drain you. But I've always *loved* bein' in the studio.

APPENDIX:
FORMS

PROJECT SCHEDULE

PROJECT NAME

SESSION #   DATE AND START TIME:

STUDIO

TUNE OR TUNES LISTED IN ORDER	TRACKS TO BE RECORDED:
	MUSICIANS/INSTRUMENTS INVOLVED:
NOTES:	☐ RHYTHM ☐ INSTRUMENTAL SOLO ☐ HARMONY ☐ VOCAL ☐ SWEETENER ☐ OTHER

BUDGET WORKSHEET

PROJECT NAME _____

STUDIO _____

PREPRODUCTION

Professional Instrument Setup
(list each instrument separately)   COST

SUBTOTAL A	$

Parts
(list all drum heads, tubes, cords, strings, spare parts,
you may need to purchase for each instrument listed above)   COST

cassette(s) (of what you have in mind, to be given to the engineers	
lead sheets	
SUBTOTAL B	$

BUDGET WORKSHEET

PROJECT NAME _____

STUDIO _____

TRACKING

COST

studio sessions (multiply number of sessions by hourly rate)	
3 hours overtime (usually a higher rate)	
cost of tape for tracking	
rough mix cassettes (whether studio supplied or provded by you)	
studio instrument rental	
session players	
their equipment rental fee	
producer's fee	
SUBTOTAL C	$

BUDGET WORKSHEET

PROJECT NAME

STUDIO

POSTPRODUCTION

	COST
mixing	
editing, sequencing, tape transfers (safety and additional copies)	
mastering	
UPS or Fed Ex (both ways; to and from)	
photography (get a professional)	
graphics, layout, design, writing, editing of text, for inserts	
printing of inserts	
mechanical rights fees (minimum: $34.75 per tune for 500 units or less)	
copyright fees (your work: both phonorecord and sound recording)	
$100 to the Musicians Performance Trust Fund	
SUBTOTAL D	$

BUDGET WORKSHEET

PROJECT NAME _____

STUDIO _____

POST-POSTPRODUCTION

	COST
duplication	
distribution (factor in labeling, packing, and shipping)	
SUBTOTAL E	$
SUBTOTAL A	$ _____
SUBTOTAL B	$ _____
SUBTOTAL C	$ _____
SUBTOTAL D	$ _____
SUBTOTAL E	$ _____
TOTAL PROJECT BUDGET	$ _____

PROJECT
CHECKLIST

1 PREPARE BUDGET (see Budget Worksheet)

2 SELECT STUDIO

☐ Call studios. (Is the staff accommodating? Have they done similar projects?)

☐ Visit studios. (Can you communicate with the engineer? Is the place close at hand?)

☐ Hire or appoint producer.

☐ Select tunes for the project.

☐ Routine all songs.

3 SCHEDULE SESSIONS

☐ Book sessions (five 4-hour).

☐ Have instruments professionally set up.

☐ Prepare lead sheets.

☐ Invite engineer to a gig.

☐ Prepare project schedule (supply a copy to engineer).

4 THREE DAYS BEFORE (*each* session)

☐ Gather spare parts (and check that all other parts are in working order).

☐ Fit instruments with new strings, drum heads, reeds, etc.

☐ Make list of everything that goes to the session.

☐ Determine who will be at the session (and who will not).

☐ Confirm date with studio (inform them of any changes).

- ☐ Purchase tape (both for tracking and rough mix, exactly as specified by the engineer).

- ☐ Make a list of any questions you have.

- ☐ *Don't* change ANYTHING.

- ☐ Practice, practice, practice.

- ☐ Provide engineer with a setup chart.

5 DAY OF SESSION

- ☐ While loading up for the studio, check off every item on the list.

- ☐ Check off each item on the list while loading in at the studio.

- ☐ Get tape into hands of engineer.

- ☐ Place instruments in studio.

6 DURING THE MIX

- ☐ Provide tape(?)

- ☐ Obtain rights (to other people's works as well as your own).

- ☐ Listen carefully to all rough-mix tapes as the process proceeds.

7 PREPARE FOR DISTRIBUTION (sometime before mastering)

- ☐ Artist/band photo.

- ☐ Layout/design of inserts.

- ☐ Mailing list/labels, envelopes, cover letters, etc.

PUBLICATIONS YOU SHOULD GET YOUR HANDS ON

THE TRADES

The trades are expensive and they're not written for the musician—but you can gather information from reading them that you can't get anyplace else. Surprisingly, by simply pawing through the trades, you can soak up some real information about the music business. After a while, you'll discover that you've started to see the industry for what it is and not for what you've always hoped it to be. Insight into the workings of the business of music will always more than compensate you for any time you spend seeking it. If nothing else, reading these publications will dispel any illusions you may harbor about the industry—knock it right out of you. And you'll be better off for it.

Billboard

For more than one hundred years Billboard has been THE music industry weekly. Over 200,000 of the people you want to be doing business with have it delivered fresh to their desk each week. *Billboard* is truly what the business is about. Singles charts, album charts, information about labels and executives and distribution and group signings and who-what-all-ever-else you might need to know to be in-the-know. (212) 764-7300

PollStar

Provides an insider's current, up-to-date listing of everybody who is working at the labels. Insider news, artists' bookings, concert results, album sales charts, radio airplay charts, interviews with industry pros. (800) 344-7383

BOOKS

This Business of Music

The biggest, most complete guide to every aspect of the business end of the music business. *The* definitive tome. Covers everything you might need to know about record companies, music publishers and writers, general music industry aspects. The price is very reasonable for a 700-page book crammed cover to cover with vital information. It looks great on the shelf, and every time you crack it open you'll be impressed with the scope of the information inside. Written by M. William Krasilovsky and Sidney Shemel (New York: Billboard Books, 1995).

This Business of Artist Management

How do you get beyond playing the local gigs and get yourself headed for the big time? Pick up this book; get yourself some management. If you think you can make it in the Biz without good personal management, then you don't know what you're talking about. Read this book, and you will. Written by Xavier M. Frascogna, Jr., and H. Lee Hetherington (New York: Billboard Books, 1990).

Breaking In to the Music Business

One of the best parts of this book is the revealing interviews with successful artists. The author also covers contracts, publishing deals, how to work with management, and other important aspects of the business that the artist should be informed about. Written by Allen H. Siegel (New York: Fireside Books, 1990).

All You Need to Know About the Music Business

This book has heavy endorsement from people like Michael Eisner, David Geffen, Quincy Jones, and the President and CEO of Capital Records. Mo Ostin, Chairman of the Board at Warner Brothers Records, says, "I almost hesitate to recommend Don's book—it gives away more inside information than it should." If nothing else, this book reveals the undeniable fact that artists who hope to defend themselves in the music industry arena had better develop great math skills. An important book for the artist, written by Donald S. Passman (New York: Prentice Hall, 1991).

The Art and Technique of Performance

The only book on this important subject that I've ever found. Written for a classical guitarist readership, this small book holds some real answers to problems that any performing artist might suffer. It covers pre-concert preparation, performance anxiety, and practicing to perform. Written by Richard Provost (San Francisco: GSP Publications, 1996). (415) 386-0395

The Art of Recording: The Creative Resources
of Music Production and Audio
Offering insight into the workings of the audio engineer's mind, this book reads like 19th-century Germanic theological debate, or perhaps the very best of Samuel Beckett. Every step of the recording process is invested with dozens of real options, and the author has undertaken the task of pointing them all out. Of course, there's a certain aesthetic to reading this sort of thing. It can be extremely fulfilling (as well as informative) for anyone with the temperament for it. I guess I walked away with, possibly, 1 percent of what the man said, but was truly impressed. Written by William Moylan (New York: Van Nostrand Reinhold, 1992).

Sound Advice—The Musician's Guide to the Record Industry
I read this book when it first came out. My recollection is that most of it was over my head. (That's a recommendation.) Written by Wayne Wadhams (New York: Schirmer Books, 1990).

Music Money and Success: The Insider's Guide
to The Music Business
An excellent, extensive, all-inclusive guide to the business of the music business. Written by Jeffery Brabec and Todd Brabec (New York: Schirmer Books, 1994).

Making Money Making Music (No Matter Where You Live)
A highly readable, convincing guide to alternatives to being gobbled up by the Biz. Written by James Dearing (Cincinnati: Writer's Digest Books, 1994).

ATLANTIC and The Godfathers of Rock and Roll
This book reveals more about the business of selling records between the lines than most books written by industry pros. It's entertaining as well as informative. To read about Ertegun falling asleep while negotiating a contract with Mick Jagger is just one of many of this book's pure delights. I also like the part where the majors were in a bidding war for a group that didn't even exist. Nicely written by Justine Picardie and Dorothy Wade (London: Fourth Estate Limited, 1993).

Billboard Books also offers:

The Billboard Guide to Music Publicity by Jim Pettigrew, Jr.

The Billboard Guide to Home Recording by Ray Baragary

The Real Deal: How to Get Signed to a Record Label From A-Z by Daylle Deanna Schwartz

For a catalog of books published by Billboard Books, call (800) 278-8477.

MORE RESOURCES

Billboard also publishes seven essential reference guides to the industry that can add substantially to your knowledge:

International Buyer's Guide. The worldwide music and video business-to-business directory, with record and video companies, music publishers, distributors, etc.

International Talent and Touring Directory. Lists U.S. and international talent, booking agencies, facilities, and products.

Record Retailing Directory. Detailed information on thousands of independent music stores and chains across the United States.

International Tape/Disc Directory. All the information on professional services and supplies for the audio/visual tape/disc industry.

Nashville 615/Country Music Sourcebook. The comprehensive source for business-to-business listings in and around Nashville.

The Power Book. The ultimate guide to radio and record promotion, with listings of radio stations, record companies, radio syndicates, and the top 100 Arbitron markets.

International Latin Music Buyer's Guide. The essential tool for finding business contacts in the Latin music marketplace.

To find out about any of these guides, call (800) 344-7119.

MIX Bookshelf
This is a great source for books covering every aspect of the music business, from the business of music to recording to theory to performance. (800) 233-9604

MUSICIAN Magazine's Guide to Touring & Promotion
Contains an A&R directory, a list of publishers, manufacturers, and a touring guide. (212) 536-5248

Disc Makers
A source of various readable, *free* catalogs about tape preparation. (800) 468-9353

ADDITIONAL CONTACTS

American Federation of Musicians
1500 Broadway
New York, NY 10036
(212) 869-1330

ASCAP
One Lincoln Plaza
New York, NY 10023
(212) 621-6000

BMI
3232 W. 57 St
New York, NY 10019
(212) 586-2000

Harry Fox Agency
110 E. 59 St.
New York, NY 10022
(212) 922-3024

INDEX